SILENT LIVES:
HOW HIGH A PRICE?

For Personal Reflections and Group Discussions about Sexual Orientation

---

Sara L. Boesser

Sara L Boesser

Hamilton Books
an imprint of
University Press of America,® Inc.
Lanham · Boulder · New York · Toronto · Oxford

Copyright © 2004 by
Hamilton Books
4501 Forbes Boulevard
Suite 200
Lanham, Maryland 20706
UPA Acquisitions Department (301) 459-3366

PO Box 317
Oxford
OX2 9RU, UK

Library of Congress Control Number: 2004109502
ISBN 0-7618-2968-7 (paperback : alk. ppr.)

To my parents Mildred and Mark Boesser for their unconditional love
and boundless support.
To my sisters Kate, Barbara, and Cindy
for their devoted loyalty.
And to my partner Carol Zimmerman for her
steady love, humor, and patience.

Contents

Preface

When I first began writing *Silent Lives, How High a Price?*, it had a different title. I called it "What Price Passing?" and for it I interviewed friends and acquaintances regarding two things. First, the prices gay, lesbian, and bisexual individuals pay when they feel they must pass as heterosexual in order to feel safe and accepted; and second, the prices they saw society itself paying when it pressures people whose sexual orientation is not the heterosexual norm to hide such an integral part of themselves.

The first question was familiar to many I spoke to; but the second question was new to most. Almost everyone who is an adult today spent many years of their lives under the old axiom that passing as heterosexual—staying in the closet and being silent about one's lesbian, gay, or bisexual sexual orientation—was "best for everyone." To be asked to ponder not just the personal price paid for that silence, but the prices society paid, too, was to enter a whole new realm.

Beyond those first interviews, this book took on a life of its own as it became more and more clear to me that it was the *silences themselves*, self-imposed and societally demanded, that were harming people's lives. Contrary to the 'silence is best' mantra, it became increasingly clear that silence had an unexpectedly high price tag for everyone, not just sexual minority people but heterosexual people as well, than most people had begun to imagine. The impact of personal and societal silence was clearly the crux of what I was uncovering, and the book's title resolved to *Silent Lives, How High a Price?*

Over time, more and more people are finding themselves contemplating the far-reaching issues involved. The media, politicians, religions, teachers, counselors, parents, family, and friends—it seems everywhere people are discussing what is meant by sexual orientation, gay/lesbian/bisexual/transgender rights, same-gender couples marrying and adopting children, lesbian and gay clergy, coming out . . . the list goes on and on. Many will welcome the opportunity to move beyond debates that too often stop at the pro/con, right/wrong surface level.

Silent Lives, How High a Price? offers a path to the more intimate, the more personal side of the discussion, not just for gay/lesbian/ bisexual/transgender/intersexual persons but for heterosexual people as well. It invites readers of every sexual orientation—be they hetero- sexual, gay, lesbian, or bisexual—to deeper reflection about what it means to be a silent sexual minority person, known but not known by those around you.

Silent Lives, How High a Price? not only tells of peoples' lives and the all-encompassing challenges individuals experience when they realize they're not heterosexual, but also provides questions and exercises which can prove helpful for group discussions, for use as a textbook, for use as a therapy supplement, or as a personal reflections handbook.

For sexual minority persons, the questions posed in *Silent Lives* often have a surprising twist and take them to a new level of self- understanding. For straight friends and family who may have felt personally immune to sexual orientation issues, the questions can lead to startling discoveries. For persons who have difficulty or fear about the concept of non-heterosexual lives, the book offers a non- threatening way to move closer to the issues and begin to contemplate them within familiar contexts.

Silence about sexual orientation separates people at a much heavier price tag than most of us might have imagined. It is my hope that *Silent Lives, How High a Price?* will invite people to communicate across those silences and help hasten the day when the societal pressures which have forced so many into silent lives will become a thing of the past. I especially hope this is a book people will share with those they care about, and that the gift of moving beyond silence will be given and received manifold.

Sara L. Boesser
Juneau, Alaska
2004

Acknowledgments

This book took fourteen years in the making, and I'm grateful to everyone who urged me on and supported me through its painstaking process.

A special thank you is given to my father, who read every single version of *Silent Lives* and offered priceless insights with gentle care and wisdom. Another special thank you is given to my mother, for testifying on my/our behalf at each and every anti-gay hearing that ever came our way, showing how allies can always make the world a better place. And a forever thank you is for to my partner Carol for understanding, sometimes better than I, how writing something as deeply personal as *Silent Lives* is something my soul had to do, no matter what.

A final appreciation goes to Letha Dawson Scanzoni and Virginia Ramey Mollenkott for writing the book *Is the Homosexual My Neighbor? Another Christian View.* Their 1978 book (and its 1994 revision) became a touchstone and an inspiration in my life, and I purchased four to eight copies every year for many years to give away to people struggling with issues around sexual orientation. My hope is that *Silent Lives* will follow in its healing stead.

Credits are also gratefully given to the following for additional permissions to reprint materials: Mildred Post Boesser; Dr. Robert Paul Cabaj, M.D., Director San Francisco Community Behavioral Health Services; Dr. Andrew R. Gottlieb, Ph.D., Clinical Supervisor, Children's Aid Society-PINS Diversion Program, Brooklyn, New York.; the *Juneau Empire*, Dr. Patricia Barthalow Koch, Ph.D., Associate Professor of Biobehavioral Health, Penn State University; Virginia Ramey Mollenkott, Ph.D., author of *Omnigender: A Trans-Religious Approach*; Parents, Families and Friends of Lesbians and Gays (PFLAG), and Carol Zimmerman.

Introduction to the Author

This book is the result of my personal struggle for integrity.

The original draft was a twenty-five page paper titled "What Price Passing" written in 1990 in an effort to balance the gains and losses involved in coming out as a lesbian. I'd realized it was no longer acceptable to my sense of self to remain silent about such a major aspect of my life. To that point I'd lived secure in the knowledge I was okay regardless of culture's judgment of my sexuality, and that society was simply blind in its unwillingness to accept the full me.

So I'd tried to live an exemplary life, striving to be above reproach in everything *except* that which to me was most personal and most dear. I thought that would be enough. But I was wrong. At some indeterminable point in time, I realized I could no longer be silent and let society condemn a core part of me while praising the outer manifestations I selectively permitted it to see. And with that realization came another: while society was blind, my very silence was what blocked its vision.

From that instant of realization, my only hope for personal peace was to seek clues that could free me from my silence and to speak out about what I discovered in the process. This book is the result of the first fourteen years of that search.

Of course, who I was by the time this search began started many years earlier. In 1990, I was forty years old. The emotional juggling act I'd lived all my adult life had worn me down to the point where the struggle for personal integrity was finally central.

Until then, to socially benign inquiries such as "who are you," "what do you do," and "what are you like," for decades I'd always internally imposed unspoken qualifications before answering: where? when? with whom? The reason: ever since my late teens, I'd felt driven to hide a vital personal part of who I was, and to do so I'd had to censor not only my communication with the world, but also my engagement in it.

This meant I didn't let the full truth of my experience pass my lips; I refrained from entering conversations that might have become personal; I passed up social, religious, and professional activities; I passed up leadership opportunities; I passed over friendship possibilities. I did it all to pass as "normal," so that I could, I thought, be allowed to participate fully in life. I passed over the socially unacceptable part of myself in all public arenas. The bargain I sought was that if I did pass successfully, it'd be best for everyone—for me of course, but also for all those around me who'd be uncomfortable dealing with my truth if it came out.

What was my truth? Who was it I prevented people from knowing after this reign of silence began?

I was born in the Blue Ridge Mountains of North Carolina in 1951. I was my parents' first child, entering their life as my father became minister to his very first parish that worshiped in the small stone Episcopal church there. My parents were well-educated—my mother with a degree from Vassar in Christian education; my father a degree in physics, prior to entering the ordained ministry. They were exceptionally warm, loving people, full of joy and excitement about life and nature.

By 1955, I had three younger sisters, and our family moved to a small town in Texas. There, horses were the love of my life, and I started school and began playing sports games with my friends. My folks have a photo of me at about age four, sitting alertly in a pretty dress, holding a large colorful plastic ball. They laughingly remind me that practically my first sentence was "Frow me d' ball."

In 1959, we moved to the town that became home: Juneau, Alaska. Juneau was a magic land with its snow and mountains and water and glaciers. My childhood was full of play and adventure—singing, skiing, fishing, hiking, boating, and sports of every variety—softball, basketball, and tennis, to name a few.

I was a happy, energetic child, confident I was loved. I was fortunate to excel in both schoolwork and sports. Church activities, church camps, and choir were also ever-present. While not popular in the traditional sense, my friendly nature gained me acceptance in most social settings.

As the oldest of four girls, one might have expected me to be the role model for my younger sisters. But I was clearly a mold to only my own way of being. Perhaps the protection of being a minister's daughter staved off the sort of teasing other tomboys received. Or perhaps I was oblivious in my love of all I did. My parents lived what they preached, and they taught that I could do anything I set my mind to, and that they'd love me no matter what I chose. To that backdrop, add the tenets most dear from church—that "Jesus loves me, this I know," "God is Love," and "Where there is love, there is God," and you can sense the solid foundation I received with which to be myself in the world.

When puberty dawned, I took new teachings to heart. My parents were sincere in stressing that when my true love came, I'd know, and that it wouldn't matter if he were black, brown, red, white, or green (as in a Martian—said in only partial jest, but I believe they meant it). While I had no interest in dating boys long after even my youngest sister was going steady, I took my mother's assurances to heart. She said I'd know when the right one came along and that there was no hurry.

But as time passed, and I observed my sisters becoming more and more assured of their place in the world, I felt increasingly out of sync, increasingly conscious of being on the outside looking in at something I not only did not understand, but felt no connection to. Girl friends were less available for activities and adventures, and seemed to take on an undecipherable boy-focused language that held no allure for me; boys who had been friends suddenly stopped being buddies and moved away, into an unreachable zone where I was no longer welcome in sports or camaraderie.

It wasn't until I was seventeen that I began to put the fractured pieces of my own reality together and realized my parents' assurance that I'd know when "the right one came along" had been missing something. How could they have imagined that, yes, I'd know when the right one came along—and it wouldn't matter to me if he were . . . a she?

The revelation came in bits and pieces, each without warning. My first kiss should have been my clearest clue. I'd agreed to date an older boy—man, actually—mature in his early twenties. After a few dates in which he proved fun and a good cook to boot, he parked at a scenic lake and, after talking a while, gently kissed me on the lips. The shock that went through my body was electrifying, but not for the reasons one might expect. Rather, at the instant of the kiss, my mind jolted to the absolute certainty that I was kissing the wrong person. I should be kissing "Isabelle," a special girlfriend I was close to (the name of course is changed—she never heard this story).

Shocked at my own thoughts, I drew sharply away from my date. When he apologized for going too fast and promised profusely to be patient and go as slowly as I wanted (he was set on marrying me, for some reason I had been unable to fathom), I could only stammer and withdraw. To his pleas of what was wrong, I could say nothing. He took me home, and I never went out with him again.

My mother's intuition was on target that night when I returned home. She knew I was upset, and I sensed she was worried about me, and about what had happened. I was unable to reassure her, able only to say that all we'd done was kiss. Did she fear much worse? I only knew I dared not say more, for not only had I discovered in my very first kiss that I was kissing the wrong person, but that I was kissing the wrong gender. After the cultural preparation of a lifetime, I'd failed society's expectations mightily. But unknown to me, I had also unknowingly internalized society's other training: that such nonconforming thoughts could not be spoken of.

I had no word then for what the unsettling turn of events might mean. Since I had no language or experience to identify what had happened, and sensed it wasn't safe—even with my mother—to try to speak of it, the memory became hazy. I basically put it out of my mind, probably still sure, somewhere in my heart, that my parents' promise of the right man coming along would happen some other day.

Many months, maybe a year, later, an older friend and I were thinking ahead to my graduation from high school, and she said in passing that a lot of gay women would probably be interested in me at college. In response, I said, "What's gay?" She was clearly dumbstruck by my naiveté, and stumbled through an awkward, hurried explanation of women who cared about one another much like men and women did, who liked to cuddle together, and who sometimes made a life together.

Our conversation moved on to other aspects of college life, but that evening as I took our family dog out for a walk by myself, I played the fragment of our conversation over again in my mind.

I can remember the very spot on the dark snowy sidewalk where I suddenly caught my breath and stopped in my tracks. What filled my mind was like a thunderous "Aha!" At that instant, I knew for an absolute certainty that not only did I understand what gay meant, but I was it! The relief was overwhelming, for with that understanding I suddenly knew there was, somewhere, a place where I would fit.

When I could move again, my step was buoyant, and I felt an emotion akin to gratitude. Gratitude because, even without articulation, my life suddenly made much more sense. I felt taller, wiser, happier, and full of anticipation. But almost immediately following that moment of exuberance, almost in the same breath, came another, heavier voice, my inner knowing that said, all at once, "Yes, I'm gay, and my parents aren't going to like it. But that's all right. It will have to be all right."

The two-part message might not seem of grave import to some, but I was a child intent on pleasing my parents. It was imperative to me never to disappoint them in anything if I could help it. So, for me, the grateful discovery of my place in the world of intimate relationships coincided painfully with a sharp grief over knowing I would not, after all, be able to meet my loving parents' expectations of me. It was my first conscious abandonment of their guidance. The fact that I didn't even conceive of abandoning my self-discovery shows how resoundingly certain I was that what I had realized was absolutely right for me.

I didn't speak to my parents, or to another living soul, about my realization until after I went away to college. Halfway through my freshman year, I told my best friend, a tennis buddy, that I thought I might be gay, but that she needn't worry because I didn't know anything about how it was done. Bless her heart, she stayed my friend. My first kiss (with a woman) wasn't until my second year of college. My mother was right—the earth *did* shake, and this time not in confusion.

I didn't have my first relationship until I was twenty, and didn't attempt to "make a life with someone" until I was twenty-four. That relationship didn't survive, but today, at age fifty-two, I've celebrated my twenty-fourth anniversary with my partner Carol and am looking forward to as many more as we're fortunate enough to live to see.

When I entered the world of non-heterosexuality, I believed at first that I'd never be able to speak of it to my family or to any non-gay/lesbian/bisexual friends. That was the norm for young people in the early '70's. I experienced intense fear—fear not only of rejection, but also of causing irreparable hurt. I heard too many stories from friends, and in lesbian/gay/bisexual circles, of people who suffered tremendously when they came out—some being disowned, barred from family gatherings, or enduring other emotional attacks; while others, in their attempts for more openness, saw their parents' resulting suffering and disappointment as causing more pain than they'd intended. But the withdrawal from my family became too much for me to bear, and slowly, one by one, I did come out to them. I didn't tell my mother until I was twenty-four years old, seven years after that moment on the snowy sidewalk in Juneau. I'd never been so afraid to tell her anything, but she was wonderful. She immediately hugged me—in the middle of a crosswalk in downtown Seattle—and said that no, she hadn't already known, but she was so glad I'd told her!

In a later phone call from my father, he, too, was reassuring, saying he'd always loved me and always would, and this could not alter that. Over the next year and a half, I told my sisters, and they too were supportive and in no way abandoned me. Years later I told an aunt, years later still my grandmother, and after more years some cousins. In that time, I began to also be more open about myself to heterosexual friends, even co-workers. There, I faced not only my fears of rejection, but also fear of possibly suffering job loss or even physical violence if they inadvertently told someone I didn't know who might feel justified in harming "those homosexuals." But despite the (too often accurate) predictions of abandonment and physical danger if the truth came out, I was extremely fortunate. I suffered no physical attacks, losing a few "friends," but no close family or jobs.

Maybe it's because of my foundation of loving family and partner that I kept risking coming out more and more. I didn't do it to alienate anyone; I did it to become closer to the people I cared about. I shared that intimate secret about myself because if I didn't, they didn't really know me, and for me to act as if they did was a lie. What began to sink into my consciousness, slowly but surely, was a gradual awareness that my being "out" was a whole lot better than being withdrawn and superficial. Cultural norms would seem to predict dire results for gay and lesbian people who are fully themselves, but my experience over and again was just the opposite. Even when people did reject me, I felt better in the end because at least the relationship was real—and not based on partial truths or on assumptions that were actually lies.

And I realized another thing: as I was more open about who I was, not only was I happier, I was also more productive at work and more creative in all my personal and professional activities. It was like I'd had my light under a bushel, and while I'd thought only one aspect was dampened down, in fact everything was. As I came out, my very spirit, my love of life and my participation in it began to flourish.

At some point, I realized I'd stumbled on an antidote to a very deep hurt in our society. Being fully who we are, without passing as something else, is actually best not just for us but also for those around us. The daily pain I'd experienced around passing as heterosexual was not, in fact, a prerequisite to a good life—rather, it was a proscription against one. As that ripple of realization gathered momentum, I found myself on a wave I would not—*could* not—abandon, even at its most frightening moments. The wave is in motion toward the fullest integrity I can attain in this life, and writing this book is one way to share what has become clear to me so far.

Silent Lives is not meant to be a finished work that will withstand, unaltered, all tests of time. It is, instead, a compilation of personal experiences—my own and those of people I've interviewed—and of publication research, and opinions, and hypotheses based on all of the above. It is intended to be a window through which other insights can come to light. The interviewees spoke from the heart to tell their truths in the clearest manner they could. The publication research provides a broad spectrum of information for further reading and study. My opinions and hypotheses are based on all the facts, experiences, and intuition I am able to compile at this time in my life. I look forward to learning from the reactions to the book, and trust it will be used as a guide for understanding and a tool for healing the struggles every reader experiences regarding this issue.

The purpose of this book is to provide enough information to inspire positive, constructive dialogue across the silences that have kept people separate and afraid of one another until now. My hope is that it will enable deeper discussion, more understanding and greater trust than there has been before. I hope it provides some healing to those who have experienced or are experiencing the pain that passing as traditionally heterosexual imposes. And, most of all, I sincerely hope it moves our society in some measure closer to the day when pressure to "pass" will not be the norm; to the day when every single person clearly understands that we *all* have the world to gain in ending the oppressions that have caused the phenomenon of passing to exist in the first place.

The value of personal relationship to all things
is that it creates intimacy and intimacy creates understanding
and understanding creates love.
~ *Anais Nin*

Part One

The Personal Price of Silence:

What are the personal costs for individuals who pass as heterosexual?

1. Secret Lives: The veil of silence

Most people who are lesbian, gay, or bisexual "pass" as heterosexual almost every day of their lives in some way, shape or form. The advantages of being silent about who they really are come easily to mind: to avoid being labeled according to prevailing negative stereotypes; to avoid losing jobs, housing, friends, and even family; to escape blackmail, discrimination, and anti-gay violence. Passing as heterosexual brings safety. Passing obviously pays. But at what price? What price does the individual pay, and what price does society itself pay when people must hide in order to be safe?

The extent to which passing and homophobia (fear, dislike or hatred of people whose sexual orientation[1] is toward people of the same gender[2]) affect every single person in our country is extremely under-recognized. In the book *Is the Homosexual My Neighbor? A Positive Christian Response*, theologians Letha Dawson Scanzoni and Virginia Ramey Mollenkott carefully and clearly unveil the far-reaching extent to which homosexuality, passing, and homophobia interconnect us all. Their example is within a church setting, but it holds true for *all* groups of people. Their overview, though lengthy, shows, better than anything else I've discovered, the full picture behind society's silence on the subject:

> There are also far more people touched by homosexuality than many Christians think. Unlike gender or skin color, homosexual orientation can be hidden indefinitely. For that reason it is hard to say how many homosexuals there actually are. But educated estimates range anywhere from 2 to 10 percent of the population, counting only those whose desire focuses predominantly and habitually on their own sex, not those who have only one or two passing homosexual experiences. . . . Assuming a 5 percent incidence, in a congregation of two hundred, as many as ten persons have to sit through any mention

of the "sin of homosexuality" outwardly pretending that it does not apply to them, but nevertheless feeling rejected and hurt inside.

In addition to the pain of these hidden homosexuals, there is the pain of their parents, many of whom either know or strongly suspect the homosexuality of their children. (One homosexual Christian recently told us how his mother wept uncontrollably when their pastor had preached that all homosexuals would be consigned to hellfire; she was heartbroken for her beloved son, and he was heartbroken for her suffering as well. Yet he had not *chosen* to be homosexual, and there was no formula by which he could relieve his mother's anguish.) So by counting the parents . . . we can see that in a congregation of two hundred, the number of persons who may be directly affected by the issue of homosexuality now raises to at least thirty.

Since many homosexuals marry in order to avoid suspicion or in hope of being "cured" by the union, we must also add the pain of their spouses, who know something is wrong and who often blame themselves for not being attractive enough to their mates. Add to that number too those uncles, aunts, brothers, sisters, children, and friends who may suspect the secret and you have approximately one-quarter of the congregation.

At the other end of the spectrum of feeling on this issue, in a church of two hundred people there are probably at least a few who are filled with rage or disgust at the very mention of homosexuality. The stronger the feeling of revulsion, the stronger the possibility that the person harbors deep anxiety about his or her own sexuality. That could bring the number of directly concerned individuals up to approximately sixty in a congregation of two hundred.

But to one degree or another, *everybody* senses feelings of love for persons of the same sex, both within and outside of the family unit. If fear and confusion about homosexuality are strong enough, even common feelings familiar to us all may cause anxiety, furtiveness, and guilt. . . .

Thus there is no denying that, although homosexuals form a minority in society and a carefully hidden minority in most churches, homosexuality is an issue that cannot be brushed aside. In one way or another it directly concerns us all. (1994, pp.4-6)

What is it like, for people who realize their innate sexual orientation is outside society's currently defined norm, to live with the many silences and the outspoken prejudices surrounding who they are? In 1948 and 1953, Dr. Alfred Kinsey of Indiana University's Institute on Sex Research published findings that are frequently quoted. They indicate that approximately "one in every ten women and men is primarily or exclusively same-sex oriented in their sexual behavior" (Identity, 1986, p. 1). Researcher Amity Pierce Buxton breaks the findings down further:

> Using a zero to six point scale representing degrees of homosexual behavior on a continuum, Kinsey estimates that ten percent of men are exclusively gay for at least three years, including four percent who are gay for life. From three to seven percent of women aged twenty to thirty-five are estimated to be more or less exclusively lesbian.
>
> Bisexuality—experiencing a high degree of sexual pleasure from both sexes—forms a less definitive picture although it is a distinct orientation. Current research suggests that at least twice as many bisexual as homosexual persons exist. (Buxton, 1994, pp. xii-xiii)

Despite such findings, society continues to presume all its members' sexual orientation will be only and always toward persons of the opposite gender—that everyone will be strictly heterosexual. Society goes on to reinforce that expectation by every means possible, sometimes consciously, often unconsciously, with the assumption and its manifestations going unnoticed by the majority of people.

But for up to ten percent of the population, the assumptions raise inner discord. As is true elsewhere in the country, "on the average, gay and lesbian Alaskans first recognize their sexual orientation at the age of 12.5 years, but do not disclose their sexual orientation to others until they are 20.1 years old, a difference of nearly eight years" (Green and Brause, 1989, p. viii). At their first moment of realization, inner discord begins; in the years of confused silence that follow, inner conflict builds.

Moments to Reflect –

All readers of every sexual orientation are encouraged to consider all questions posed for reflection. Homosexual, bisexual[3], transgender[4], and intersexual[5] persons face questions like these all their lives. But in fact, often unknown to themselves, heterosexual persons too are caught up in the same puzzle of sexual self-discovery and self-understanding usually only verbalized for non-heterosexual, transgender, and intersexual persons to ponder. As people of all sexual orientations engage in dialogue on questions such as these, many will be surprised to see the similarity of experience every human faces, knowingly or not, with regard to sexuality, silences, assumptions, issues of difference, and more.

1. "Despite . . . findings, society continues to presume all its members' sexual orientation will only be toward persons of the opposite gender: that everyone will be heterosexual."

    a.   What untrue assumptions do strangers tend to make about you? Which assumptions do you choose to correct? Which do you leave uncorrected? Why?

    b.   What untrue assumptions do friends and family tend to make about you? Which assumptions do you choose to correct? Which do you leave uncorrected? Why?

    c.   Does your significant other tend to make untrue assumptions about you? Which of these assumptions do you choose to correct? Which do you leave uncorrected? Why?

    d.   Do you think strangers ever assume you're "straight" (heterosexual)? If so, what conscious or unconscious signals do you think you're making to send this message? If their assumption is incorrect, are you comfortable correcting them?

    e.   Do you think strangers ever assume you're gay, lesbian, or bisexual? If so, what conscious or unconscious signals do you think you're making to send this message? If their assumption is incorrect, are you comfortable correcting them?

f. Are you aware of yourself checking for others' sexual orient-tation? Always? Seldom? How do you think you do it? Why? How do you feel when you're unsure?

2. "As is true elsewhere in the country, 'on the average, gay and lesbian Alaskans first recognize their sexual orientation at the age of 12.5 years, but do not disclose their sexual orientation to others until they are 20.1 years old, a difference of nearly eight years.'"

   a. As a child, did anything major affect your life that you kept secret from *everyone* for five or more years? How did keeping that secret feel? Who did you finally tell? Why?

   b. If you did not have this experience of many-year, self-enforced silence, can you imagine what it might have felt like?

   c. If you are a parent, can you imagine your child keeping an exciting, welcome experience or discovery from you for eight years? How would that feel to you? What if it was a difficult, stressful experience or discovery they kept from you?

In general, all readers are encouraged to consider all questions. Only in a few selections, such as the following one, are questions broken out according to readers' sexual orientation for additional focus. In most sections one set of questions provides the essential focus for everyone. Bisexual persons may wish to reflect on both sets of all questions, since they are generally perceived as heterosexual if with an opposite-gender partner, and perceived as homosexual when with a same-gender partner. Throughout this book, bisexuals are included with the gay men and lesbians questions, because bisexuals generally suffer the same societal attacks as gay men and lesbians when others discover the bisexual is not exclusively heterosexual. And, throughout this book, transgender and intersexual persons are invited to read the sections that fit their orientation—be it opposite-sex, same-sex, or bisexual.

3. "But to one degree or another, everybody senses feelings of love for persons of the same sex, both within and outside of the family unit."

3-1 *For heterosexuals*:

   a. Think back through your life. Who were your closest same-gender friends as a child? As a young adult?

   b. What qualities of these same-gender friends attracted you to them?

   c. Do you have close same-gender friends today? What qualities attract you to them?

   d. Is it easy to maintain your same-gender friendships? If not, what are the challenges?

   e. Think back through your life to same-gender friend(s) you have or had who did not conform to typical "male" or "female" behavior or appearance. How old were you? What qualities attract(ed) you to them? Is/was it easy to maintain the friendship(s)? If not, what are/were some of the challenges?

3-2 *For lesbians, gays, and bisexuals:*

   a. Think back through your life. Who were your closest opposite-gender friends as a child? As a young adult?

   b. What qualities of these opposite-gender friends attracted you to them?

   c. Do you have close opposite-gender friends today? What qualities attract you to them?

   d. Is it easy to maintain your opposite-gender friendships? If not, what are the challenges?

   e. Think back through your life to opposite-gender friend(s) you have or had who did not conform to typical "male" or "female" behavior or appearance. How old were you? What qualities attract(ed) you to them? Is/was it easy to maintain the friendship(s)? If not, what are/were some of the challenges?

2. What is the price for children who realize they are "different"?

Even at twelve and a half years of age, children know for certain that they are outside the norm if they have strong feelings about children of their own gender. Despite common misconceptions, their interest is not a "choice." Twelve-year-olds would not voluntarily choose behavior that would subject them to abandonment by their peers or to interminable pain and harassment.

Instead, what actually happens is that one day, with absolutely no preplanning, an individual suddenly realizes that his or her body is sexually reacting to that of another human being. No one chooses when that sexual energy magic happens. It just happens. The sexual-energy response happens first. Then slowly, but surely, the individual realizes she or he is oriented to being sexual—with someone.

For one child, it can begin as simply as daydreaming continually about a certain person; for another, it might be the sudden tingle when someone accidentally touches his or her hand; for yet another, it can be an intense friendship, or an extreme depression when a special friend moves away. Experiences of this new-found intensity build on one another until eventually a young person realizes that the feelings are sexual attraction. If the young person looks out and recognizes the object of his or her desire is of the opposite gender, no second-guessing occurs, for they'll be labeled the norm: *hetero*sexual.

But if she or he looks out and finds the object of their desire is of the same gender, alarm bells go off, for they recognize they're not being the norm; society will label them as *homo*sexual (or bisexual)[6]. Not unlike a compass swinging north, their body, on its own, has found its sexual interest oriented toward the same gender. They didn't set out to find sexual energy coursing through their body that day, that moment, at age twelve (or eighteen or twenty-five). They simply recognized the attraction they felt. No choice was involved.

At the realization that they'll be labeled homosexual, many children tend immediately to withdraw, enforcing a self-imposed isolation on themselves so they won't be found out.[6] Despite the fact that the American Psychiatric Association declared homosexuality a normal variation of human sexuality back in 1973 (APA, 1974, 131:4), these children have already heard years of the hateful prejudice people express about "those homosexuals"—the emphasis being on the discardable "those," as in those dangerous others, those who are not welcome, those who are undesirable—those who are not us: *those* homosexuals.[7]

The children realize they don't fit the stereotype, but are helpless to seek comfort or support for fear of absolute rejection. From their distanced withdrawal, they seek safety and learn "to pass." That is, they learn how to speak, move and check for clues of safety and danger in everything they think, do, and say. Quickly, they realize their safety and *acceptance as people* is based on lies; thereafter their socialization is based on deception. Passing as heterosexual becomes paramount; and spontaneity, dangerous. Constant self-monitoring becomes the key to successful social interaction.[8]

Sometimes sexual minority* youth cannot keep their secret and find themselves at a severe disadvantage for how to cope. Ethnic- and religious-minority children usually experience their minority status from birth, but they usually also experience, from birth, support and

---

* "Sexual minority" is sometimes used as a kind of shorthand when the entire list of "lesbian, gay, bisexual, transgender, and intersexual" is what is being referred to. In *Silent Lives,* sexual minority means gay, lesbian, or bisexual people who are a minority due to their consensual sexual orientation status; transgender persons of any sexual orientation who are a minority for feeling they were born into the wrong gender's body; and intersexual persons who are a minority since their bodies aren't clearly "male" or "female" by society's binary body-sexing standards.

The term "queer" as a positive non-pejorative statement of self-identification is not included in the sexual minority listings in *Silent Lives,* in large part because those who self-identify as queer don't always also self-identify as gay, lesbian, or bisexual. Readers who self-identify as queer are invited to read the sections that fit their orientation—be it opposite-sex, same-sex, or bisexual.

"Sexual minority" does not include transvestites (those who cross-dress but are comfortable with their birth gender), and it does not include any other sexual behavior differences (such celibacy, pedophilia, etc.).

modeling from similarly-situated adults who can offer skills and emotional support for surviving attacks from the majority culture. But the unexpected revelation of one's sexual minority status can shatter a youth's life physically:

> Gay youth are the only group of adolescents that face total rejection from their family unit with the prospect of no ongoing support. Many families are unable to reconcile their child's sexual identity with moral or religious values. . . . They are more often forced to leave their homes as 'pushaways' and 'throwaways' rather than running away on their own. . . . Gay male, lesbian, bisexual and transsexual youth [youth who believe they've been born into the wrong sex's body, feel trapped, and wish to become the opposite gender] compromise as many as 25 percent of all youth living on the streets in this country. (Gibson, 1989, pp. 3-112)

At school, those who are known or suspected of being non-heterosexual (oft-times called "queer"[9]) can expect harassment that is frequent and often harsh—sometimes even violent. The strain can cause youth to have few close friends and experience extreme isolation.

> The shame of ridicule and fear of attack makes school a fearful place to go, resulting in frequent absences and sometimes academic failure. [One study found that] 28% of his subjects were forced to drop out because of conflicts about their sexual orientation (ibid., 3-112, 113).

Every time I read a news account of a young teen or college undergraduate who commits suicide despite "having it all: good grades, good looks, good family, good future," my stomach drops. There are many possible reasons people speak of for such tragedies—among them bad drugs, bad music, possible untold sexual abuse, or mental illness. But what I have to add to the list is the teen's possible self-realization, or accusation by others, of same-gender attraction: their fear of being homosexual in a homophobic world. I personally have been called to a local hospital by a teenage boy who attempted suicide after telling his mother he was gay—and her immediately throwing him out of his home "forever."

Many of my adult sexual minority friends tried or seriously considered suicide at a young age. A published federal study[10] found that gay and lesbian and transgender teens, and teens who are questioning their sexual orientation, are two to three times more likely than other teens to attempt suicide (Gibson, 1989, pp. 3-122/3). All non-heterosexual youth are at high risk. And for some, the burden has additional weight:

> Ethnic minority youth (i.e., Black, Hispanic, Asian, and American Indian) compromise a substantial number of the youth who are gay, lesbian, bisexual or transsexual. . . . Ethnic minority youth face all the other problems that other gay and lesbian youth face growing up in a hostile and condemning society. They also . . . have tremendous fears of losing their extended family and being alone in the world. This fear is made greater by the isolation they already face in our society as people of color. These ethnic minority youth who are rejected by their families are at risk of suicide because of the tremendous pressures they face being gay and a person of color in a white homophobic society. (Gibson, 1989, 3-122/3)

There are two additional groups of youth who may or may not be homosexual or bisexual[3], but who can also be at higher suicide risk because they can experience the same mistreatment aimed at those perceived as sexually outside the "norm." These are *transgendered*[4] (or transsexual) youth, those who from birth believe they were born into the wrong gender's body and wish to live as or become the opposite gender (Gibson, 1989, pp. 3-124), and *intersexual*[5] youth, those born with physical properties of both sexes (Holmes, 1995).

The transgender person's inner struggle is with their own body, because their body does not match the gender identity[11] they know themselves to be within. What may begin as dressing and behaving as the gender opposite to their physical body many progress years later to include the choice of surgical and/or hormonal methods to physically change genders and make their body match their internal perception of self.

Intersexuals get the message from outside themselves that their body is wrong, as doctors and family often choose not to accept a body which isn't traditionally male or female. Sometimes the ambiguity of gender is evident at birth and multiple "corrective" surgeries and hormonal regimes are done to select and impose a clearly male or clearly female body for the intersexual—in a process out of the intersexual child's control. Common medical practice has been to keep secret from the intersexual person the real reason for early and ongoing medical procedures, attempting to spare any unease or uncertainty about their sense of gender identity. In many cases it's not until many years later that the adult intersexual becomes aware exactly what has been done to them or why they've experienced so much medical focus on their anatomy.

For others, early medical intervention is avoided because only at puberty does their sexual ambiguity become evident. And others won't realize their intersexual status until later still, or even at all, unless a medical condition arises that causes them to discover their apparently-male or apparently-female body actually has qualities of the gender that doesn't match their outward experience. For example, for some intersexuals-unaware, their intersexual status may only come to light "when they attend a fertility treatment clinic in later life as they struggle to have their own children." (Mollenkott, quoting Whittle, 2001, p. 45).

But for anyone, at whatever age their intersexuality becomes evident, the resulting negative reactions of others can be a major impact, as can be confusion about one's self. What to do, who to be open with, who to trust all become intense challenges.

Both transgendered and intersexual youth may struggle about their true gender identity (not necessarily accepting the physical gender received at birth or by surgery), and may feel painfully out-of-place or isolated. Their sense of isolation and of irreparable difference from their peers can make them feel suicidal, too, even at a very young age.

For example, Oprah Winfry interviewed a young mother whose eight year old son had always dressed as a girl and played only with girl toys, and had told his mother "God made a mistake" when he made him a boy. The mother tearfully told Oprah her son had announced to his second grade class that he was a girl trapped in a boy's body. And she said he told her:

> Mom, it's like when God put a baby in your stomach, it was a girl. But then, when you prayed for a boy, God changed me into a boy. And that's why I'm all messed up. . . . Mom, I hate getting shots worse than anything in the whole world. But I wish God could give me some medicine in a shot that could make me act like a boy, and have boy thoughts. I want to act like a boy but I can't help myself. Mommy, it's like I don't want to live. [12]

This young child could express himself better than many, and he was fortunate his mother offered love and compassion in response. But peers and family often harshly condemn children who don't comply with traditional gender role behavior. The prevailing stereotype is that nontraditional gender-behavior is a forerunner to becoming gay or lesbian, so these children often suffer anti-gay harassment even if many will later go on to be heterosexually attracted to the opposite sex.

It shouldn't come as a big surprise that anti-gay prejudice is behind many of the attacks both transgender and intersexual children suffer at very young ages because of their behavior or body differences.

In the Oprah Winfrey show "Why does my child act like the opposite sex?" Oprah asked the distraught mother of the eight-year-old outright, "What is it you really want to know? Do you want to know if you're raising a gay son?" The mother tearfully said she'd love her son no matter what, but so far he's said he's not gay, and she wants to believe him. Oprah and several counselors spent time explaining the difference between gender identity and sexual orientation to the parents on the show. But it was clear that for most, an underlying fear was that their children, if they continued to cross-dress and act as the opposite gender, would have much harder lives because they might turn out to be gay or lesbian.

And for intersexual newborns, one underlying reason behind the early intervention surgeries is the doctors' and parents' stated hope to remove any question about a child's gender, so the child can have a "normal life." Into normal, I read "not homosexual." Why? Because of the teasing and harassment anyone who looks sexually different is apt to receive. Because society's knee-jerk inclination would be to shunt anyone sexually different into the only familiar subset they know—the "homosexual others" subset of sexuality. If society were not so afraid of consensual sexual behavior differences (homosexuality), then sexual body differences might not arouse the fierce medical alteration efforts intersexuals endure.

Some transgender and intersexual youth, in addition to their emotional distress over their own physical discord, do eventually also recognize internal same-gender attractions. If, when they do become sexually aware, they do find themselves attracted to someone of the same gender then they will find within themselves a double challenge to society's expectations: both transgender and intersexual people (1) know gender itself is changeable and/or uncertain in a society that has traditionally assumed gender to be "clear cut" and "given"; and (2) they realize their additional gay, bisexual, or lesbian status will forever make them prey to the attacks society aims at non-heterosexual people regardless how they may eventually resolve their physical body status. The challenges can feel insurmountable.

So many suicides, the ultimate price of personal pain, show us that too many gay, lesbian, bisexual, transgender, and intersexual young persons' efforts to fit society's gender "norms"—in their attractions and in their own bodies—do not relieve their anguish, nor does whatever degree of passing the sufferers employed. For too many of these youth, pain can feel unbearable, and they come to believe death is their only solace.

Of course, most gay, lesbian, and bisexual youth, and most transgender and intersexual youth who may or may not be homosexually or bisexually oriented, do survive. I spoke to a number of adults about their experiences*.

When I talked to Paul[13] about his childhood, he recounted recognizing his sexual orientation in the third grade. "The thing that's amazing to me about my youth is how creative I was. My imagination was so 'out there.' From third grade until at least ninth, I isolated myself and lived in total fantasy to escape." During that time, he recalled, "I had many opportunities to go out in the woods with the boys, and do sexual things boys do, but I turned them all down, for fear they'd know I liked it, for fear they'd know I was gay." What price does he feel now that he paid then? "The price I paid when I actually did socialize was that I couldn't reveal my feelings. And I was fearful all the time that they'd find out I was gay."

Isaac's realization came earlier still. "I knew from when I was a young child that I was gay, but I thought I was the only one. By first grade I knew I liked boys and I knew nobody else did." For him, the realization was a heavy, always-looming burden: "How did it feel? I just knew I had a secret that I couldn't tell anybody about. And whenever I got in any kind of trouble—through my entire childhood—I thought that somehow they knew the secret." What did he think the repercussions might be if his parents found out? "I guess maybe I thought my parents would disown me if they knew. Even at age seven somehow I knew it was very bad; and as I got older I thought it was very sinful."

---

* I interviewed a number of friends, acquaintances, and friends of friends in 1990 while preparing to write a paper titled "What Price Passing?" Each interview was about an hour long and followed a list of questions intended to get people to reflect upon the personal impacts passing as heterosexual had on their lives and on the lives of people they loved, and upon the societal impacts they saw created by society's insistence on passing.

In the book *Intersex in the Age of Ethics; Ethics in Clinical Medicine Series*, a woman reflects that she knew from early on there was something different about her, too, but the adults' silence around her about her intersexuality left her totally adrift,

> [There was always] total and complete silence. You know, it was never, never mentioned. And, you know, I mean . . . I know you know what that does. And I was just in agony trying to figure out who I was . . . what sex I was. And feeling like a freak, which is a very common story. And then when I was 12 I asked my father what had been done to me. And his answer was, 'Don't be so self-examining.' And that was it. I never asked again [until I was 35]. (Preves, 1999, pp. 56-57)

Anne recalls first realizing she was attracted to a girl when she was in fifth grade. "But before that . . . I can remember one little thing. I was eight, or seven maybe. Kay [another girl] and I kissed on the lips, and I *really* liked that. Shocked the hell out of me! Lips were up here and I had feelings down there." Anne spoke to no one of her same-gender attractions until ninth grade, and only then to another girl she discovered had similar feelings.

When asked how carrying such a secret affected her all those childhood years, Anne said,

> It's when I started being watchful about everything I said and did. . . . It felt kind of awful. I remember waiting for when I might be attracted to boys. Never did. Finally having someone to talk to, well, I wasn't alone! It was a huge thing to know that what I was feeling was felt by other people. Like a door opening up. Everything else was still hidden, closed. Totally, totally closed, off limits. Fun and freedom to be myself were very closed.

Later, in high school, a father of one of her friends frequently supplied liquor to the neighborhood girls. Anne remembers he used to say, "You'll never find Anne under the table." She says, "That sort of sums it all up. I couldn't even be drunk all the way. I had to be in control *all the time*. I could be bombed and it [not letting it slip she was gay] never left my mind—except if I passed out."

I can see everywhere
Pain invisible
I can see everywhere
Pain unfold.
How can we live it?
Pain inescapable
How can we ease it?
Pain untold.

No place of safety
No place to find peace
No trust to soothe us
Ne'er does pain cease.

We pass for our safety
Our price to exist
What gain in this passing
Save avoiding death's kiss.

~ Sara *Boesser, 1990*

Reflections—

Guided Meditation: Discovery
for group or individual

[Narrator reads the following:]

Make yourself comfortable; and close your eyes. This exercise is designed to take you back in time, back to your earliest beginnings of consensual sexual awakenings, back to who you were first attracted to, i.e. to whom you were first oriented toward being sexual with.

You won't have to share these memories with anyone unless you choose to. This journey is to remind us we're all in this together. We all undergo a sexual realization process: the first feelings a mystery, the time and place and person an unchosen surprise.

First a reminder: the sexual awaking process is just that—a process. Who we were first attracted to may or may not turn out to be the gender we actually become involved with as a youth or later in life. Attraction to both genders is normal for many young people, and fantasy about both genders is normal for youth and adults of every sexual orientation as well. Your first crush may or may not turn out to be the gender you'll find yourself in a long-term relationship with some day. The process of early realizations is what's to be experienced in this meditation. How realization . . . just . . . happens.

Now I'll ask a few questions for you to contemplate silently regarding how it first dawned on you which gender (or genders) you were attracted to—oriented towards—very early on. Take these slowly. Pause to think about each question.

As a child in school, whose books did you want to carry? Who did you want to sit beside? Whose touch was it that sent a thrill through your body? Who did you want to write love poems to? Who did you first kiss (a child-like peck on the cheek, very young)? What's the youngest you can remember any of these tinglings of pre-sexuality?

Keeping your eyes closed, now picture your first major crush – the one where you first realized the energy you were feeling was somehow sexual. Remember that first recognition of being "turned on." Remember how it just happened, and you recognized it as something new.

Now picture the face of that crush you were attracted to. If you were oriented toward someone of the opposite gender, consider yourself fortunate, because as a general rule you could move smoothly past that moment of recognition into all the socially available possibilities for young straight couples: dances, church groups, dating, dinners with the family, and talking to your friends.

Or if you found yourself oriented toward someone of the same gender, was the moment of recognition smooth? If not, what caused it to be difficult for you? What thoughts or fears came upon you at that moment?

Still with your eyes closed:

If you now consider yourself heterosexual, again picture the face, the gender, and the body of your first strong crush. If the person was the opposite gender, change that face and change that body, for just a moment, and see that person as the same gender as yourself. Try to imagine for a moment that you found yourself oriented toward—turned on by—someone like you, and try to imagine that surprise, or that shock.

What if John had been June? Or vice versa? For just a moment try to imagine: how does that feel? What would your parents say? Could you tell your friends? Could you tell even the person you're attracted to? Can you think of any supportive people or organizations that would have welcomed your realization?

Or, if you now consider yourself homosexual or bisexual, and your first strong crush was same-gender, try to imagine for just a moment how different that moment might have been had the person been opposite gender? What different activities might the two of you done? Who might you have felt free to talk to that you didn't back then?

All right—open your eyes.

Any reactions you'd like to share? Write about?

Two *Discovery* points: Realization and Process:

The preceding guided meditation exercise was provided to help us all consider two main points:

1) *Sexual discovery realization:*
      Young people realize one day, pretty much out of the blue, that they're feeling sexual energy and that it's focused toward someone, of some gender. Not unlike a compass swinging north, their body, on its own, becomes aware of a focal point of sexual interest.
      That's sexual orientation: who they're oriented to being sexual with. It precedes behavior. It just is. No choice of day, time, or person is involved.
      If young people look out and see the object of their desires as opposite sex, no pause occurs because if they act on that orientation they'll be labeled heterosexual and society is set up to welcome their realization. They'll find many socially acceptable avenues to experience, experiment, and display, or "flaunt" their sexuality.
      But if the young person looks out and sees their attraction is same-sex, they know, without knowing how they know, that they're in danger, that they must be careful who to tell, and that if they act on that orientation they'll suddenly become "other:" *those* homosexuals (and *those* bisexuals).

2) *Sexual discovery process:*
      Sexual discovery is a process that unfolds within each of us. Before it starts we can't plot or predict our path.
      For example, my sisters and I each had our own sexual discoveries. I certainly didn't choose to have my discoveries be different than theirs.
      Regardless whether it was our genes or our upbringing (nature or nurture) that lead to our discoveries, by the time they happened,

they happened. Over time my sisters' discoveries solidified so they recognized their heterosexuality; over time mine solidified so I recognized homosexuality.

With those realizations in hand and heart, no choice was available to any one of us except whether to be true to our realizations—our orientations—or not.

3. What is passing's price as individuals continue to grow?

"We are your family, your co-workers, your friends—you love us already" are the words I carried on a sign in 1987 when I marched in Washington DC for equal rights for all, regardless of sexual orientation. It's a message to the world that gay, bisexual, and lesbian people know to be absolutely true.* But because people can suffer when they dare to share this truth, many silently pass.

> They do not wear their stigma on the surface, where it is immediately obvious to all who care to look. . . . This ability to pass is a mixed blessing; in opposition to the rewards it provides, it creates the con-

---

* In many locations throughout the balance of *Silent Lives*, I will list "gay, lesbian, and bisexual" as the group under discussion.

My intention is that persons who are transgender or intersexual who know themselves to also be homosexual or bisexual will be understood to be within the list, since most of the discussion is about people under attack because of their same-gender attractions/relationships (i.e., gay, lesbian, or bisexual orientation).

Since many transgender and intersexual persons experience life with a *hetero*sexual orientation, they aren't always included each time I list out groups because they're not faced with the anti-gay element of attack as far as their intimate relationships go.

However, many other societal anti-gay-based attacks happen regardless of relationship: they're aimed instead against people with a gender identity that doesn't match their body (transgender), or against people whose physical body's gender looks different than most male or female bodies (intersexual). As a result, in some cases I do specifically include transgender and intersexual persons in lists under discussion. Please use your discretion to internally correct any inadvertent misses I might make in this effort.

stant anxiety of one who lives under a fragile construction of lies (Green and Brause, 1989, in Jandt & Darsey, p. 3).

For me, by 1987, to live under a "fragile construct of lies," no matter how great the need, was a price I felt was too high. I was raised to be honest; I wanted more than anything to have personal integrity.

For many, many years I'd tried to live an exemplary life in all ways *except* where my sexual orientation could become an issue. I thought that would be enough, that I could be at peace with myself.

But I was wrong. Every time I caught myself causing or allowing someone to think I was heterosexual, I felt sick. I was beginning to verbalize the prices I'd paid, cautiously, carefully, mostly with other lesbian, bisexual and gay friends. And I began to ask them for their insights. They, too, often could recognize prices they'd paid—in relationships, with their family, with friends and co-workers, and in their employment and careers.

Examples are endless; the following few only scratch the surface.

Relationships

Grace, now involved in a ten year lesbian relationship, who had married at age twenty-one and stayed married for over twenty years, remembers intense crushes on girls she had when she was in her early teens. She suffered a long, deep, deadening depression in high school when a girl she had a major crush on began dating boys. Grace attempted to pull herself out of the depths by trying to take an interest in boys, too. Eventually, each beau would say she was cold and responseless, even though they still liked her a lot. When she finally married a man who would've been too distressed if she'd said no, she rarely enjoyed sex and she believed she was frigid. At the birth of her first son, she asked the doctor to check and see if she had "all her parts." She reflects,

> It was terrible. I paid a price: duty-bound to perform sexually. I had to act all the time. Being unfulfilled was terrible; I didn't talk to anyone. Even so, I didn't have any idea, even at thirty-four or thirty-five, that there was such a thing as 'a lesbian.'

Allen, unlike Grace, did know early on that gay people existed. Now he's thirty-three, in a seven-year committed relationship with a man. But as a youth he didn't act on his same-gender attractions, and instead struggled to "do the right thing." Athletic, he found himself automatically in the more "jock" cliques in school. He was aware of boys he thought might be gay, but didn't risk getting to know them because his peers badgered them so mercilessly. As a young person, he recalls, "I just don't ever remember having an urge to have a girlfriend. The only reason I had a girlfriend all through school was because that was the thing to do." But as he got older, and girls pressed him for more sexual intimacy than he was willing to offer, he felt worse and worse about himself. By the time he was eighteen, he felt the price was too high:

> I felt like I used those girls, you know, because they put their love and trust in me. And here at the same time I'm having these other feelings [for boys] and telling the girls something different. And I just didn't feel good about it. I just felt like, 'No, I can't do this; I have to look for something else.'

Family

Joan feels she paid the highest price, passing, with her family. By not being as open with them as she is in work and other social settings, she realizes she's paid the price of not being understood, of having unspoken assumptions go by that aren't true. Also,

> I probably could've been closer to my younger brother, who is also gay, if it'd been out in the open. But neither of us knew. It probably cost him more than it cost me, in support [she regrets missed opportunities to be the sympathetic ear and confidant she'd been earlier on in their lives, learning only later about hard times he'd been going through]. So by not being open we lost each other's closeness.

Isaac didn't tell his parents he was gay until he was forty-five. Gratefully, they were supportive, but he initially decided not to tell his two older brothers because he "figured it was none of their business: they don't have to talk about their heterosexuality, so why should I have to talk about my homosexuality, you see?" But one brother's unexpected death changed his mind. "That's why I finally told the other

brother, that's still alive, because I didn't want him kicking the bucket
without even knowing me."

Loss of intimacy with family members is a recurrent theme for
many people. Joan now knows her brother is gay, but he hasn't told
their parents yet. She sees his greatest price in the family as being

> not to be true to himself. . . . to just have to talk about things maybe
> in a more general way, instead of being specific and saying 'this is
> what's going on for me.' I can tell he gets really frustrated talking
> about his life, because he ends up kind of putting everything together
> and saying 'I'm doing great.' You know? Instead of saying, 'This is
> what's going on here, and this is going on here.' And we all have so
> many things going on.

Barbara took another tack with her family,

> I'm 'out' to every damn last one of them. But I did tell them over
> time—safest first, and worked my way along. Initially, I did pay
> a price with my family. When one of my sisters got into the
> Jesus thing, we had only cursory contact for a long time.

During a hard time with another sister, Barbara refused to go to the
sister's wedding. Things have been resolved since, the communication
lines are back open, and she acknowledges with a smile that "the 'I'm a
lesbian and you'd better like it' chip on my shoulder is past."

Friends / Co-Workers

Despite the untrue prevailing stereotypes that homosexuals are
dangerous, scary, undesirable people, most pass as heterosexual so
convincingly because, in truth, the overwhelming majority are
conventional, law abiding citizens who do not stand out as "different"
because their only actual difference is the gender of the person to whom
they may be attracted.

The self-imposed isolation gay, lesbian, and bisexual individuals
took shelter in as children extends into adulthood, with co-workers and
often even friends being unaware of the "fragile construct of lies" the
person is juggling. Whether or not to trust people with whom they
really are, whether or not to "come out of the closet" and let others

know of their sexual orientation is an ongoing process that affects them endlessly:

> The 'significant others' lesbians and gay men must make coming-out decisions about include virtually every person with whom they have some sort of relationship or significant contact—parents, sisters and brothers, and other relatives, friends (both gay and non-gay), co-workers, employers and supervisors, landlords, neighbors, clergymen, medical or mental health providers, employees of businesses or services they patronize, etc. . . . Depending upon the significance of the relationship, and the potential negative consequences of coming out, decisions about whether or not to tell another are frequently characterized by stress, guilt, and fear. (Green and Brause, 1989, p. 2)

Whom to tell, when to tell, how to tell—why tell at all?—are endless inner struggles. It boils down to: "Who can I be myself with? Who can I be honest with? Who can handle this piece of information about me? Who will continue to be my friend if they know? Who do I care enough about to risk letting them know me this well?"[14]

Health

Hesitance in coming out to physical and mental health care providers is common. To the extent that any kind of stress can aggravate or even cause some health conditions, the constant stress of passing as heterosexual has costs that, while hard to quantify, are extensive nonetheless.

Enduring medical doctors' presumed-heterosexual questions such as, "What form of birth control do you use?" with evasion or "little white lies" is hard enough; even filling out forms asking questions such as, "Who should be contacted in an emergency?" can cause unease if the person to be listed is one's same-gender partner.

Despite the medical profession's ethic of confidentiality, far too many lesbian and gay people have had bad medical experiences, have felt their heterosexual cover endangered during some medical interaction(s) in their lives, or know of someone who has. The untrue stereotypes of us as dangerous, scary people precede us to medical services; it's not unusual to find doctors "going cold" or referring patients to other doctors when the truth does come out. Sometimes in the process confidences are broken, and people end up losing jobs, even health insurance, when news of their non-heterosexual orientation gets out.

It's no accident that so many of the original AIDS clinics and services were formed by lesbian, gay, and bisexual people: the traditional medical establishment too often turned patients away, not because of the extent of their illness (which was difficult enough), but because the patients were "those homosexuals," and were not viewed as desirable—to work to heal or even to be around.

To avoid uncomfortable interactions or possible outright rejection, withholding one's non-heterosexual orientation can seem paramount even when addressing relatively minor health conditions. As a result, sometimes only partial health histories are shared, to the detriment of optimal care. And often, visits for medical assistance for any kind of illness are postponed longer than is advisable to avoid risking compromising one's heterosexual cover.

> Fewer than half of gay, lesbian, bisexual and transgender adults disclose their sexuality to their health provider, according to new survey on gay health.   . . . 'We are dismayed to learn how the closet puts gays and lesbians at risk in speaking honestly with their doctor or primary health care provider,' said Darin Johnson, Vice President of Witeck-Combs. 'Stigma and the potential for discrimination has, for years, been a major obstacle for lesbians and gays seeking appropriate health care.'
>
> 'This survey is an important wake-up call for the medical establishment,' said Kathleen DeBold, executive director of the Mautner Project, a national lesbian health organization. 'We all know that disclosing your sexual orientation to your health care provider is extremely important to obtaining the best health care, but the majority of GLBT people are not going to do that unless we feel safe and respected in the health care environment. This survey shows that if doctors and nurses are truly committed to providing the best care to all their patients, they need to increase their awareness of and sensitivity to the needs and concerns of their GLBT clients.' (Witeck-Combs Communications/Harris Interactive Survey, 2002)

Distrust of medical care is heightened even more when it comes to mental health counseling. Successful therapy is contingent upon clients being open and honest about their lives; but openness and honesty are in direct opposition to passing.

Among people I know who do seek counseling for some issue in their lives, the work of finding a counselor who is "safe" is arduous.

Generally, many friends are consulted to find out, "Is so-and-so homophobic? Do they understand the pressures of my double life? Will they guard my secret? Will they treat me like anyone else—to help me to accept who I am—and not condemn me for being gay?"

Finding a counselor who won't add to the weight a bisexual, gay, or lesbian (or transgender or intersexual) person already shoulders can seem daunting, especially during the times of stress or crisis that often bring a person to seek counseling in the first place. So, regardless if a person's depression and/or anxiety are related to surviving in a homophobic world or not, seeking mental health care is often avoided. The end result? Physical health, mental health, relationships, job performance—so many issues that counseling exists to ease—can go unaddressed when people feel it's more important to ensure their passing than to seek help.

Employment /Careers /Volunteer Work

Since as of 2004 there are still no federal laws prohibiting job discrimination against homosexual, bisexual, intersexual, or transgendered people[15], the choice of careers and types of community involvement can also be affected by individuals' need to pass.

While many gay and lesbian people have successful, high-paying jobs (the average salary of respondents to the Alaskan Identity's *One In Ten* survey showed lesbian and gay respondents' average salaries to be $22,905 for women and $28,275 for men, with eighteen percent making less than $18,000 and eighteen percent making over $40,000 per year), research shows that higher-paying jobs tend to require individuals to be more "closeted"—to pass more—than lower paying jobs:

> These data may . . . reflect the often-discussed 'underemployment'
> syndrome in that many people who are completely out may reconcile
> themselves to jobs that, while having relatively low prestige and
> poorly paying, nevertheless do not require them to conceal their
> sexual orientation. Thus, there is some evidence here that socio-
> economic status and being out are in conflict. (Green and Brause,
> 1989, in McKirnan & Peterson, p. 5)

Joan is one of the higher-paid Alaskans I know, and her story supports the probability that many of the high salary survey respondents aren't out and open about their lives. For her and her partner she reflects:

> As for ourselves, going public would probably mean losing our jobs. I am in a business whose major clients have been very clear in public that they are adamantly anti-gay . . . . While my colleagues accept us as a family at office functions, there is no doubt in anyone's mind that the clients would call the shots if we chose to be less discreet in public. I'd be out of a job in a minute. My partner has a public job in a sensitive area where politics, not compassion, would determine her future, and the political situation for lesbians who aren't discrete is not very safe.

The concept of "not very safe" takes many forms. I personally know three people, locally, who lost their jobs when co-workers discovered their sexual orientation and told anti-gay employers. I know of another out young gay man who has been consistently passed over for advancement (though he trains everyone who passes him by) whose boss told him it wouldn't "look good" for the company to have a high profile man who "wasn't more traditional and married" (read: not gay).

I know a woman, a licensed professional with extensive experience and credentials, who successfully negotiated a job selection process and was offered a good job out-of-state. She was delighted to have been found most qualified, and to receive the job offer. But to be on the safe side (or if not safe, at least forthcoming), she wrote the company and, after thanking them for the offer, said she wanted to let them know she was a lesbian in case that presented any difficulty for them. She hoped, in it being the late '90's, to receive a "no problem" reply; instead the response was a curt withdrawal of the job offer and a "never mind" letter of rejection.

I know, too, a woman who has a good job with young people, who has been told by her boss that her sexual orientation is not a problem for the company, but if any parents found out and had a problem with it, she'd "have to be fired." And I know of a woman who was blackmailed for quite a few years by a co-worker. In her case, the co-worker threatened to tell both her parents and her boss her secret if she failed to meet his demands. She didn't want to risk the possible fallout from either front so she paid the blackmail fee, staying silent and hoping nothing worse still would happen. I could go on; the list of just those that I know of is far, far too long.

To know of even one person who has lost a job or been blackmailed puts fear of similar maltreatment into the hearts of every non-heterosexual who hears the tale. I'm fortunate to have survived almost two decades now being out and open at the job and in my public and private life as well. But to get to my initial coming out point, I had to reach the point of being willing and able to risk losing everything. For me, that was better than the internal price of hiding any longer. But everyone must weigh and balance when and if that time is right for them.

Volunteer community service, such as involvement in political or non-profit work, is also often avoided by bisexual, gay, transgendered, and lesbian people.

Barbara, for example, once thought of volunteering to be a big sister, but decided she didn't want to go through the excruciating questioning enforced in our town at that time upon people who admitted openly to being lesbian or gay. The untrue stereotype that homosexuals de facto are also child molesters is still encoded in many people's minds, despite all the evidence that *well over* ninety percent of child molesters (pedophiles) are *hetero*sexual men (as evidenced by the fact that one in four girls is sexually abused before she is eighteen, with the majority of the men who abuse them being trusted heterosexual men in their lives such as a father, a stepfather, a cousin, an uncle, a grandfather—and many heterosexually involved fathers/stepfathers/etc. abuse both girl *and* boy children).[16] Barbara says she felt the big sister organization's sexual orientation questions were "none of their business," but remembers "feeling bad for not following through and being a big sister, because a kid would've been lucky to have me."

Religion

Religious involvement is also difficult for many. Grace explains: "What price have I paid? The possibility of exploring a church here in Juneau. I'm very much held back by the fact I'm lesbian, because I don't want to be a fake and I don't want to be honest, to be seen as some kind of weirdo."

Many gay, bisexual, and lesbian people feel like Grace—their spiritual life is strong, but they find no organized religion to welcome them. Others compromise and choose to attend temple or services or mosques regularly, keeping their personal lives hidden, passing as heterosexual and bracing themselves for the anti-gay condemnations they must endure and must find healing for elsewhere.

Fortunately, some are "out" and work openly within their communities of worship trying to bridge the gulf between traditionally anti-gay interpretations of religious texts and the real lives of the lesbian, gay, and bisexual members today who are living in the midst of their spiritual communities. And, fortunately, their efforts are paying off as more and more denominations and selected branches within faiths are actually welcoming gay, lesbian, bisexual, and transgender persons into their religious communities. But even these open doors have their limits, as in the many churches, synagogues, etc. that welcome gay, lesbian, and bisexual members but would never allow someone who is out and open about their non-heterosexual life to become a consecrated leader in the faith.

Speaking for myself, as a minister's daughter, it's given me some small solace to recall my Christian roots and, however painfully, find in them hope for a day when Christianity and other religions will actually welcome the whole me. I recognize and respect the fact that many people understand the Bible from strictly their own personal perspective, which for them is true and right. I only wish they could see that my understanding of the Bible has equal merit, and is right for me. Fortunately I'm not alone:

> We would like to uphold another Christian view, quite different from the one voiced [in a recent article]. There is a growing consensus among medical personnel, many Bible scholars and Christian theologians that true homosexuality is neither a sickness needing to be healed, nor a sin needing to be forgiven, nor is it some kind of bondage from which one needs to be delivered, but rather sexual orientation is a given, a part of who one is, and not a 'chosen lifestyle.' Which is to say that sexual orientation is a part of one's created giftedness from God, whether homosexuality or heterosexuality. . . .
>
> In other words, there is an increasingly widely supported Christian view which takes the Bible, Christian theology and morality with utmost seriousness and believes that homosexual persons have a full and equal claim with all other persons upon the love, acceptance and protection from discrimination of both church and society. (Boesser, Rev. Mark and Mildred, *Juneau Empire*, September 26, 2002)

To those who sincerely say that Bible passages "can only be interpreted one way," I can only respectfully disagree. And history is on my side.

Bible quotes were used by devout Christians for far too long to support slavery and later to maintain "separate but equal" education laws and poll taxes against people of color. Interracial marriage stayed illegal in parts of America until 1967 in large part because of Bible passages used to oppose it. In Biblical times polygamy (having more than one wife) was not considered sinful as it is today (Wink, 1996, p. 9); rather, it was a divinely accepted institution in certain cultural contexts. Bible passages were the mainstay denying women the right to vote or to have equal education opportunities. Just a few years ago, Bible verses traditionally used to attack and diminish people with physical or mental disabilities were still obstructing efforts to secure equal rights and equal access for Americans who experience disabilities.[17]

In all those cases, the words in the Bible never changed. But over time, through history, religions' understanding of the *meaning* of the words changed. So today, to me, it's painful but no surprise to hear Bible quotes used against me and people like me. But I'm confident that thoughtful evaluation and prayerful reflection will enable yet another evolution to take place in Biblical understanding, this time to full acceptance of same-gender orientation and behavior.

In the meantime, I'm grateful to those spiritual communities and individuals who do welcome lesbian, gay, transgender, bisexual, and transgender persons, I honor those persons who can work from within their unwelcoming religious communities for a better day, and I grieve with those who find themselves bereft of what had once been a supportive mainstay in their lives before they realized they were no longer welcome as they truly are.

I'm also saddened when I hear genuine concern from some religious people who fear that any societal fair treatment of homosexuals might intrude upon their faiths. Their fear, fortunately for us all, is unfounded, because the legal stipulation of separation of church and state in America is present in part to protect both the religious and secular realms from differences they have with one another. As with all civil rights laws, the secular law of the land and the laws within religions are distinct, and are not enforceable upon one another.

Thus churches would not have to welcome homosexual, bisexual, or transgender members or clergy, even if civil laws were passed to grant job protection for all, regardless of sexual orientation/identity, because the separation of church and state grants churches the special legal right to discriminate *within the practice of their religion.*

That's why, for example, religions don't have to allow women to be ordained even though job discrimination in the civil arena prohibits discrimination on the basis of sex. Religions can even discriminate on the basis of religion. For example a Christian does not have to hire a Muslim to teach Bible classes at a church-funded school. Christians can't demand all commerce stop on Sundays, nor can Jews keep government services closed on Saturdays.

Even in Canada, where in 2003 the Supreme Court determined civil marriage for same-sex couples was legal due to Canada's Constitutional Charter of Rights and Freedoms law, churches specifically can still refuse to marry same-sex partners, just as they can refuse to marry opposite-sex partners for a variety of reasons (some require conversion to their faith before performing a marriage, for example).

So, to all who are devout in their faith, and fear that civil laws protecting bisexual, transgender, gay, and lesbian people might some-how intrude on their religion, it's only necessary to step back, view the larger picture and observe that, already, *within the confines of their actual religious activities*, they are free to follow their beliefs regardless of *any* civil rights, present or future.

Of course if a religious group chooses to wave the separation of church and state, as in cases where a religious organization chooses to accept public money for a program it provides, then in that particular program with public money the religious group may no longer be allowed to discriminate. But that acceptance of public money—and the accompanying requirement to adhere to all public civil rights protections for the spending of that money—is a choice a religious group can weigh and decide to make or not. No one forces them to move to an arena where they have to be more welcoming than their doctrine proscribes.

But to try to force the entire public realm—everyone outside their religion—to uphold a particular religion's beliefs about who should or should not receive equal protection forces too many people in the secular arena to live in fear of losing their jobs and careers. And that is *not* necessary for any particular religion to flourish.

The American dream of "liberty and justice for all" is sadly and needlessly undercut when anyone outside a religious setting is hired or fired on any basis other than their ability and their qualifications to do the work. The gender of one's significant other (being gay, lesbian, or bisexual), or one's nontraditional internal gender-identity (being transgender), or one's non-traditional body gender-configuration (intersexual) does not affect job performance. Living silently in fear of discrimination, blackmail, harassment, and even violence *does* affect not only job performance but one's entire life.

Questions for Reflection –

4. "It boils down to 'Who can I be myself with? Who can I be honest with? Who can handle this piece of information about me? Who will continue to be my friend if they know? Who do I care enough about to risk letting them know me this well?'"

    a. What kind of secrets *do* you share with people you come to know and care about? Why? Has sharing your secret(s) ever backfired on you?

    b. What kind of secrets *don't* you share with people you care about? Why? How does keeping the secret(s) feel?

    c. How might your life be different (better? worse?) if you did share the secret(s)?

5. "Joan knows her brother is gay, but he hasn't told their parents yet. She sees his greatest price in the family as being 'not to be true to himself. To just have to talk about things maybe in a more general way, instead of being specific and saying, 'this is what's going on for me.' I can tell he gets really frustrated talking about his life . . . .'"

    > In the following scenarios, imagine having to speak only generally to someone you're in regular contact with (a family member, co-worker, sports buddy, synagogue or church member, etc). Speak so generally that you say nothing that could even hint at your sexual orientation (heterosexual, bisexual, lesbian, or gay).
    >
    > In other words, *no* clues can be given about the gender of the person to whom you are attracted or with whom you are having an intimate relationship. How does this feel?

    a. Tell the story of a vacation you took with a significant, intimate person in your life using no name and no gender pronouns.

    b. Tell your mom or dad about a date using no gender pronouns.

    c.   Help a friend out with advice about their relationship problems, without referring by name or gender to any of your own relationships.

    d.   Talk about your goals in life without ever mentioning your significant other.

    e.   Your significant other is home recuperating from a serious illness. How will you ask your boss for the needed time off work without mentioning the reason for it?

    f.   Your significant other just won a romance trip for two to Hawaii. How will you tell people about your upcoming vacation?

6.   "Speaking for myself, as a minister's daughter, it's given me some small solace to recall my Christian roots and, however painfully, find in them hope for a day when Christianity and other religions will actually welcome the whole me. . . . To those who sincerely say that Bible passages 'can only be interpreted one way,' I can only respectfully disagree."

    a)   If you are or once were a religious person, can you remember back to things being different in your faith when you were younger than they are today? (Examples: when no synagogues or churches ordained women; or when the Southern Baptists used to ordain women but no longer do.) What other examples come to mind? How do you think the changes came about? How do you feel about changes to religious understanding?

    b)   Think about other changes in religious interpretation from long ago. For example, how it took the Catholic church over three centuries to forgive and exonerate Galileo, who the Vatican condemned to permanent house arrest for heresy because he claimed the earth revolved around the sun, in opposition to the church's biblical interpretation that the sun revolved around the earth. Or how some early honored Biblical leaders had more than one wife (what we would call illegal polygamy today).

What other religious interpretation changes took place long ago—in every faith (Jewish, Islamic, Christian, Buddhist, etc.)?

How do you feel about changes to religion that happened before your lifetime? Compare those feelings to how you feel about changes that are or seem to be in process now.

Do you think the long-ago changes were easy for people back then?

Exercise: Biblical Prohibitions

The following is a short journey through biblical reinterpretations many of us may have been unaware of. For those who today sincerely anguish about shifting their feelings about homosexuals because some Bible texts are interpreted as calling homosexuality "an abomination," see the short *Biblical Prohibitions* exercise below:

The following is from lesbian columnist
Deb Price's book, *And Say Hi To Joyce*:

An engineering professor is treating her husband, a loan officer, to dinner for finally giving in to her pleas to shave off the scraggly beard he grew on vacation.

His favorite restaurant is a casual place where they both feel comfortable in slacks and cotton/polyester-blend golf shirts. But, as always, she wears the gold and pearl pendant he gave her the day her divorce decree was final.

They're laughing over their menus because they know he always ends up diving into a giant plate of ribs but she won't be talked into anything more fattening than shrimp.

Quiz: How many biblical prohibitions are they violating?

- Well, wives are supposed to be 'submissive' to their husbands (I Peter 3:1).
- And all women are forbidden to teach men (I Timothy 2:12),
- wear gold or pearls (I Timothy 2:9),
- or dress in clothing that 'pertains to a man.' (Deuteronomy 22:5).
- Shellfish and pork are definitely out (Leviticus 11:7, 10 [abomination]),
- as are usury [loaning money at interest] (Deuteronomy 23:19 [deserving of death]),
- shaving (Leviticus 19:27),
- and clothes of more than one fabric (Leviticus 19:19).
- And since the Bible rarely recognizes divorce, they're committing adultery, which carries the rather harsh penalty of death by stoning (Deuteronomy 22:22).

So why are they having such a good time? Probably because they wouldn't think of worrying about rules that seem absurd, anachronistic or—at best—unrealistic. Yet this same modern-day couple could easily be among the millions of Americans who never hesitate to lean on the Bible to justify their own anti-gay attitudes.

After reading the previous exercise, how does it feel to know there are numerous abominations and other Biblically condemned practices most of us engage in without a second thought? An abomination is "deserving of death" in the Bible (Ezekiel 18:10-13). With that the case, if you've ever had shellfish, for example, you're as harshly condemned in the Bible's text as you would be for homosexuality.

So how do you make peace with yourself, spiritually, knowing you're breaking some of the Bible prohibition listed above which seem to condemn you? Can you imagine homosexual and bisexual persons likewise making peace with themselves spiritually when faced with texts which likewise seem to condemn them?

Curriculum Exercise: "Exploring Sexual Orientation"

The following is a curriculum titled "Exploring Sexual Orientation" created by Dr. Patricia Barthalow Koch in 1987 when she was Assistant Professor in the Department of Nursing at Penn State University:

Purpose:
Too often when the topic of sexual orientation is dealt with, the only orientation which is examined is homosexuality. Such constant scrutiny of this particular orientation tends to reinforce the idea that it is 'abnormal' or 'strange' while heterosexuality is simply taken for granted as 'the way to be.' Therefore, the following teaching aid is recommended in order to foster increased learning and understanding about sexual orientation. By first having students examine heterosexuality, the following concepts can be explored more fully:
1. We know little about the cause(s) or development of any sexual orientation.
2. Stereotyping or labeling is unfair and harmful.
3. There is more to a person than his/her sexual orientation.
4. People are people; our similarities are greater than our differences.
5. All people have feelings.

Audience: High School, College, Adult.

Procedure:
The following list of questions should be handed out to every individual. The exercise is most effective if students are given time to really think about the questions and process their thoughts and feelings. Therefore, giving these questions in the form of a written assignment to be discussed later in a small and/or large group format is a most beneficial learning experience.

Goals:
1. To gain more information about sexual orientations, while recognizing the lack of knowledge in this area.
2. To uncover misconceptions and stereotypes in relation to sexual orientations.
3. To explore one's own feelings, beliefs, and values regarding sexual orientation.
4. To become exposed to other people's points of view, attitudes, and values.
5. To develop an ability to empathize with others.

Questions:
1. What is heterosexuality? (Define)
2. How can you tell if someone is heterosexual ('straight')?
3. What causes heterosexuality?
4. Is it possible that heterosexuality stems from neurotic fear of others of the same sex?
5. The media seems to portray straights as preoccupied with (genital) sex. Do you think this is so?
6. Do you think straights flaunt their sexuality? If so, why?
7. Do you believe it is sinful for straights to engage in sexual behavior with other than vaginal/penile intercourse for pro-creation?
8. In a straight couple, who takes the dominant role and who takes the passive role?
9. If 50% of married couples get divorced, why is it so difficult for straights to stay in long-term relationships?
10. Considering the consequences of overpopulation, is it feasible that the human race could survive if everyone were hetero-sexual?
11. Since 99% of reported rapists are heterosexual, why are straights so sexually aggressive?
12. A disproportionate majority of child molesters are heterosexual. Therefore, do you consider it safe to expose children to heterosexual teachers, scout leaders, coaches, etc?
13. What would you do if a straight person of the other sex tried to force him/herself on you?
14. When did you choose your sexual orientation?
15. Did one of your teachers have a significant influence on your sexual orientation?
16. How easy would it be for you to change your sexual orientation starting right now?
17. Techniques have been developed which might enable you to change your sexual orientation if you wished to. Would you consider intensive psychotherapy? Aversion therapy? Electro-convulsive therapy? Prefrontal lobotomy?
18. What have been your reactions to answering these questions? What *feelings* have you experienced? Why?

Now, look over these questions again. Substitute the words 'homosexual' for 'heterosexual,' 'gay' for 'straight,' 'other sex' for 'same sex,' etc.

4. How does it feel? What personal price is paid?

Interestingly, when the people I interviewed were asked to reflect on the personal price they had paid for passing, their initial responses were often hesitant and, even if not slow to come, were definitely not immediately extensive. Perhaps because they had not often, if ever, been asked to verbalize their silent internal struggles, each person at first seemed to find it difficult to examine themselves and see where the gains and losses fell out.

But since "passing" has a more generally recognized context of African-Americans passing as whites, especially before the "Black Pride" and black civil rights movement, I also asked them what price they felt was paid/is paid by those individuals.

When Caucasians were asked how they felt African-Americans might have suffered then, or suffer today, to pass as white, the light bulbs visibly went on, and each person listed *many* of the following, often followed with asides of recognition of the same issues in their own lives: loneliness, fear of blackmail, coercion, isolation (especially from family), "*really* hard to be 'on stage' all the time," a waste of "a lot of energy that could've been spent on better things," depression, fear of loss of job or home, fear of how life would be worse if you're found out, and confusion about where they fit.

When I interviewed an African-American (heterosexual) woman who had been actively involved in the early black civil rights movement in order to get her perspective on the passing of blacks as white, an unexpected reversal took place. Initially she, too, didn't have an immediate extensive response for blacks, but did have a ready visible concern for the pain and price gay and lesbian people pay. She stated firmly that:

The price is personal hypocrisy. People have to live with themselves. For blacks, or for gays and lesbians, the hardest person to live with is yourself, and when you know, deep down, you're lying, you do more damage to yourself than to anyone else.

Despite the fact that it's actually society's hypocrisy (i.e., society's insistence on maligning its racial minority and non-heterosexual members) that leads people to create their fragile construct of lies in order to feel safe or to be able to keep or seek a certain job or religion, etc., the internal discord of even "successful" passing can cause damage and does cause pain.

Joan believes "the world works better on truth. [Having to pass] affects my degree of optimism of whether the world will ever work as I hope it will—operating on openness, not assumptions. Passing adds to the fabric of falsity we've weaved about a lot of things."

Another thread of falsity is the "cover" people sometimes seek in specific social settings. It is not uncommon, periodically, for a gay man to go on "dates" with a lesbian friend or acquaintance—both of them intentionally choosing to be seen together publicly in order to pass as a heterosexual couple for family, career, or other purposes. Company gatherings, family reunions, and religious events can present frequent pressure for a traditional date.

Paul sees lesbian and gay people dating one another in order to pass

as creating an anxiety level I'd prefer not to have. There's all that fake touching crap. Even if you're friends, it's a facade, not real. And, nine times out of ten, you give up respect for yourself. I feel so sorry for people who do that.

In general, as Barbara put it,

The price [of passing] is a matter of pride—the price you pay is losing pride. Like, you catch yourself saying or doing something, a choice of a pronoun or adjective. And sometimes the pretending comes too easy. And that hurts, too.

Of her early 20's, Anne says,

I thought of myself as very good at deception, and I developed the attitude that I didn't care about what other people thought. 'Resentful' is a good word for it. I deceived, but I was resentful about it, resentful of having to do it. To build my self-esteem, I was proud of my deception ability.

Now, from her present beyond-forty perspective, Anne speaks vehemently of passing:

I don't like it; I never did. I hate it! It's the worst thing in my life. And I can say that from the very beginning: I never liked it, ever. I never got comfortable with it, ever!

By age forty-two, Grace knew:

I realized I was dying inside. And I would die emotionally, totally, if I didn't do something about it. Being authentic is what I want, to be at peace with myself—to have my own internal self fit with the external self.

5. How would people be different if they didn't pass?

When I explained to one friend that I was exploring the price paid by both individuals and society by so much passing, she asked tentatively, "What do you mean, exactly? If I didn't pass, how would I be different? Would I look any different, talk any different, act any different? What do you mean by 'not passing'?"

I readily explained that people wouldn't look or act any different, that what I meant by not passing was that it would no longer be necessary to have our guard up, to have to double-check everything we think before we say it, and that by no longer spending so much constant energy monitoring ourselves we'd be free to be more creative and more fully involved in *living*. She sounded relieved.

Later, reflecting back on our conversation, I suddenly realized how sad it was that her question even had to be asked. But I knew it was an important one. Many people somehow fear that if lesbian, gay, and bisexual people are fully themselves, they'll somehow overnight become exceedingly different. That isn't the case. The fact that we pass so well is because we are so similar. Perhaps the most noticeable initial difference will be much more verbal than visible. Bisexual, lesbian, and gay people would finally be free to be spontaneous, able to interact genuinely in activities and feel free to talk about their lives.

The conversation reminded me of a discussion I had with a woman who was putting together a panel of participants to describe their perspectives of suffering discrimination as minority people. She said she was considering having a person on the panel cover the sexual orientation issue. She said, however, that she "didn't want to blow peoples' socks off with a flaming gay," and I did an involuntary backstep.

While she hadn't actually used the all-too-common derogatory epithet for gay men, "faggot," my internal reaction was as strong as if she had, because the term "flaming gay" brings to memory the Middle Ages when homosexuals were burned at the stake with fires started by bundles of twigs called faggots.

Her unintentionally harsh choice of words is an example of people fearing that if lesbian or gay people speak at all about their lives, that they'll somehow be "flamingly" different. Coming face to face with such expectations often makes it easier to pass than to be honest and come out.

6. How do lesbian, bisexual, and gay people feel about famous / successful people who pass?

Lesbian, bisexual, and gay people intimately understand the multitude of reasons why people choose to pass; thus, most are very hesitant to fault people who do. When asked how they felt about famous people who miss opportunities to end negative stereotypes about homosexuals by passing, opinions varied.

Joan:

> I'm not convinced they could make a difference [in ending the negative stereotypes]. I feel famous people shouldn't be forced to say they are, because the press will force them to make that [their orientation] their issue, and they might want to do something else. Homophobic folks affect my life, not the ones who stay in the closet.

Paul, however, feels very differently:

> How do I feel? Angry. It pisses the shit out of me to see people who have the power to change opinion but don't do anything. They should at least contribute money—heavily [to groups working to end sexual orientation discrimination]—if they just can't come out.

Says Anne,

> Three years ago I would've thought, 'Great, get away with what you can.' But now I think differently because I'm out, because of pride, and not being ashamed of who and what I am. Liberace—I hate him 'cause he went out there, gay as hell, and yet he wouldn't come out. [18] And he was accepted and loved by all.

Part Two

The Fabric of Our Lives:

What are the Costs to Society?

7. What are the ripple effects when people pass?

When a sizeable portion of society lives in daily fear of loneliness, rejection, and violence, not just those individuals, but everyone connected to their lives, pays a price. And everyone is interconnected, much more than we'd expect. With the research figure of one in ten in hand:

> If you know 50 people, chances are you know at least five [who are lesbian, bi, or gay]. Chances are you probably know, deep down, that at least one of them is 'that way.' Maybe she or he is a fishing friend, a fellow student, or someone in your church. Maybe he or she is a relative. (Boesser, Sara. *Juneau Empire*, 1988)

The personal cost to individuals extends, however silently, to an almost endless extent, with society paying prices it creates but is unaware of. As with individuals, specific examples are endless. The following few scratch the surface.

Family as a social structure

What societal price first came to mind for those I interviewed? Several people saw society's price *to the family* as the most extensive cost.

Anne points out:

> The family's price extends throughout society. If we can be honest with our families, they could be honest with their relatives. The dis-

honesty [of passing, of lying] is extended through and beyond the
family. The family price is a *huge* one—it's the biggest.

Joan, who initially stated, "I haven't paid a price by passing;
what someone does [in private] isn't supposed to affect that," came to
see, through the window of the price paid by African-Americans who
pass(ed) as white that

> for family [that knows, but keeps it secret from others], the price is
> really high. Lots of discussions and energy go around trust and
> disclosure that could have been spent on other things.

Alice, a heterosexual woman, bemoaned the price of silence within
her family as she explained that soon she'd be going to an extended
family reunion of up to forty people, some of whom she knows to be
gay, but that within her family *no one* is to speak of the subject. She
feels sorrow because one of her gay cousins has AIDS, and has been
near death several times already. He'll be at the reunion, and she aches
for his having to maintain the charade they are all expected to carry out
—not admitting his illness or making any allusion to his real life. The
entire family (those who know but say nothing, and those who don't
know but sense something is wrong) will suffer from the undercurrent
of unspoken secrets and will carry that pain away, back into their
everyday lives.

Loss of family support during times of health crises can be
traumatic for everyone involved. The desire to call on family and
friends to talk about one's illness, or the need for a helping hand during
a bedridden episode, is something anyone can experience without
warning.

But when one isn't out to family or friends, she or he may be
unable to invite them into their confidence or into their homes, not just
for AIDS but for *any* illness. If they're passing as straight and have
talked of a partner only as a "roommate," they may feel unable to invite
helping hands over to what turns out to be a one-bedroom apartment, or
even to a larger home, if they believe the roommate could be viewed as
"obviously" gay or lesbian. As a result, even in severe emergencies,
family members may be kept in the dark through the entire situation, or
may be called in only if death seems imminent.

If family does find out about the medical crisis afterward or some
time into it, they can experience confusion and distress about not being
included earlier; some may feel cheated of a chance to assist. To add to

the stress for all involved, if they come to realize in the midst of the health crisis that their family member is unexpectedly *not* heterosexual, some may become angry, and during or after the emergency may reject the family member outright.

None of these scenarios are desirable. The person who is ill passed so well for so long to avoid just such family turmoil and grief. But with illness upon him or her, passing's guard may have to fall, and the additional stress of coming out during crisis can greatly compound the seriousness of the situation for the person who's ill and for her or his relatives.

Sometimes it turns out that the stress of passing, itself, causes ill health, as in the following example where a man had married in hopes it would make him straight:

> [hiding one's true orientation—often from oneself as well as from a spouse] can also lead to severe physical problems or self-destructive behavior such as alcoholism or suicidal feelings. One husband who married thinking his graduate school [gay] affairs were behind him suffered severe chest spasms eighteen years later. As he hovered near death, his wife took him to several doctors who were unable to determine the cause. Undergoing further treatment including massage, rolfing and Reichian therapy, he finally revealed what had been buried in his frail chest. After he disclosed his homosexuality, he left the doctor's office pain-free. (Buxton, 1991, p. 205)

Of course, while the husband felt new freedom, his spouse's resulting shock and their journey to re-evaluate their lives had only begun[19]. But at least they'd avoided his early death, and could then, both together and individually, face what lay ahead.

There's a striking failure in health care that society's anti-gay stance and individuals' passing join together to impose at the worst possible times in people's lives, one that causes incredible distress and potential long-term grief. It's this: only spouses and "immediate family" are automatically allowed in a patient's emergency care hospital room.

For most lesbian and gay couples, legal civil marriage is not yet possible.* Imagine being kept out of your partner of many years'

---

* Only the Netherlands, Belgium, and three Canadian provinces allow same-sex couples to legally marry as of early 2004, with Sweden and Massachusetts poised to follow suit later that year.

hospital room as she or he struggles for life after a serious accident. Or imagine being the patient, attached to tubes and machines, unable to speak for yourself, wondering where your partner is and wanting him or her beside you.

Many same-gender couples take out powers of attorney to ensure hospital visitation rights. And in a few states, and in some jurisdictions, laws or policies have been passed to give same-sex partners hospital visitation and other rights. But when doctors and family haven't been notified as to whom one wants present in emergency situations, the time it takes to locate the necessary partnership document can be too long. A price of passing, of not having come out sooner or for being unable to come out during the emergency, can be loss of vital support for the patient, and sometimes even the lost chance to say goodbye if the partner dies.

For family who didn't know and later learn that they'd unintentionally kept their relative's loved one from the bedside, a tremendous range of emotions can result: anger at him or her for being non-heterosexual or at themselves for not knowing; dismay and sadness for obstructing someone's needs at the end of life; or guilt about why they didn't know or for having blocked comfort.

Even family members who intentionally intercede and knowingly refuse admittance to the same-gender partner can experience emotions like these. It's not uncommon for people to deny and strike out against their relative's homosexual or bisexual orientation when they first learn of it, yet then over time to come to terms of acceptance about it. But when someone has died, it's too late to make personal amends. The resulting sadness or guilt can be a heavy burden.

Society pays in other family arenas, too. Youth suicide is crushing not only to immediate families, but to school friends as well. Too often, one youth's suicide leads to another's and another's. So when one youth takes his or her life because they fear rejection or failure due to their same-gender or transgender or intersexual awakenings, other young people are at risk regardless of their sexual orientation. And in reverse, the suicide of a heterosexual young person can be the only trigger another youth needs to take his or her life when they're struggling with questions about their orientation or their gender.

Teen pregnancy is another grave family concern nationwide. In Alaska for instance, one in eight teenage girls is pregnant. How does homosexuality fit into teen pregnancy? How better to "prove" to your friends that you're not homosexual than to get a girl pregnant, or to become pregnant? This is a well-known phenomenon among gay and lesbian people. For example, in one Minnesota study lesbian and bisexual public school students age twelve to nineteen were found to have "approximately twice as great a prevalence of pregnancy . . . as either unsure or heterosexual young women" (Saewyc et al, 1999). Sometimes the pregnancy is just a way to pass; other times the young person sincerely hopes parenthood will make her or him "straight" (heterosexual). Either way, a child is conceived by teenagers unready to raise a family, and society pays in many ways to attempt to compensate for another teenage birth.

Not just pregnancies, but many marriages, too, are sadly colored by people who feel such passing is absolutely necessary in order to survive and be successful. Innumerable marriages thus take place in order for a woman or man to "prove" s/he is not homosexual or in their hope that marriage will provide a "cure" to their homosexual attractions. Others hope the marriage will provide enough of a "normal" involvement for them to become successful, while still having some same-gender relationships on the side to fulfill those longings.

> Most homosexual or bisexual persons don't want to be rejected for belonging to a minority which Judeo-Christian society historically has stigmatized as unnatural, immoral or criminal. Many people therefore deny or repress feelings of attraction to the same sex. . . . [For those who choose to marry], whether they are aware of their homosexuality, deny it, or consciously hide it, they want to have children and the security that marriage affords in a society that values the family. While they may genuinely love the woman they marry, a study of gay husbands . . . suggests that internalized homophobia and social pressures are significant factors in their decision to seek marriage. . . . Many believe their love is strong enough to make them forget, if not overcome, their sexual orientation. (Buxton, 1991, pp. xii-xiii)

Isaac's story reflects this belief perfectly. He married in his early twenties, was married twenty years and raised two children with his wife before acknowledging that he was too much at war with himself to stay in the marriage any longer. Why did he marry initially? Though he realized he was gay in first grade, he became "very religious" as a way to fight off his feelings. At age nine he sought out the Presbyterian church, and led his entire family to baptism there. But by college, despite his determined dating with women whom he truly liked as friends, and his constant church activities, he realized his feelings for men were getting even stronger. He reflects that he was desperate to be both a good Christian and heterosexual. In a desperate effort to cure himself of the "abominable feelings," he first decided to convert to a "stronger" religion and joined the Catholic church. When that didn't end his attractions to men, he concluded marriage would. And everyone supported him in that decision:

> [Before we married] we talked about it, Alicia and I, about that I was gay. And we went to the psychiatrist and to the priest and we went to counseling, and we really were told, 'well, we think you guys can make it!' You know, we definitely believed in that 'and they lived happily ever after' fairy tale story. And that there wouldn't be these feelings, or that the feelings wouldn't be important. The important thing would be the marriage and the relationship. I had no idea that it would still be with me twenty years later. I just kind of thought this [marriage] was the magic formula to make me heterosexual.

The mistaken idea that such marriages might possibly work is often the tragic result of the myth that homosexuality is an illness or a "choice," and that if people just decided to, they could be cured and/or could "choose" to be heterosexual.

The American Psychiatric Association officially ended the myth that homosexuality was an illness or a choice when, in 1973, it removed homosexuality from the APA list of mental illnesses. In its "Position Statement on Homosexuality and Civil Rights," the APA declared, "Homosexuality per se implies no impairment in judgment, stability, reliability, or general social or vocational capabilities . . . [and] no burden of proof of such judgment, capacity or reliability shall be placed upon homosexuals greater than that imposed on any other persons" (APA, 1974, pp. 131:4). Dr. Robert Paul Cabaj, M.D., a former Chair of the Committee on Gay, Lesbian, and Bisexual Issues of the APA, explains:

> Sexual orientation—heterosexual, homosexual, or bisexual—is a basic part of a person's nature. . . . In other words, sexual orientation is normal and natural to that person, and homosexuality, therefore, is a normal variation of human sexual expression. A person does not choose sexual orientation; it is a basic part of his or her nature. (Cabaj, 1990, p. 1)

My own personal clarification is this: "orientation" is an innate, subconscious "chemistry." Every person has an orientation, made evident by whatever set of external stimuli "turns them on."

In other words, no one can choose who they'll become attracted to: no one can flip through a phone book, point to a name, and say, "When I meet this person, s/he will be physically/sexually/emotionally attractive to me." Instead, one's attraction response is far beyond such conscious selective behavior.

What happens instead is definitely magic: an internal, involuntary reaction occurs in response to some person, where one suddenly realizes her/his sexual interest is oriented in the direction of that particular person.

Orientation has thus already happened instinctively. All one has available after finding him/herself oriented in a particular person's direction is the decision as to how to behave in response to that orientation. When persons choose to act in the direction they find themselves oriented, if they become sexually involved with others who are attractive to them, then they have chosen to be true to and to act on their involuntary orientation.

People make choices about acting on their orientation responses continually. Even people in committed, monogamous relationships can on occasion find themselves attracted to (that is, oriented with sexual attraction to) other people. To remain monogamous, they choose not to act on their attractions. Their behavior is a choice; their orientation (finding certain additional people attractive) is not.

When a man finds all his attractions—all his orientations—are toward women, or a woman finds that all of hers are toward men, such people can say their *orientation* is heterosexual. If they choose to act on their orientation, and become sexually involved with some person(s) of the opposite gender, they can also say their *behavior* is also heterosexual. Their external behavior was a choice, but only after internal orientation had become evident to them.

When a woman finds all her attractions—all her orientations—are toward other women, or a man toward other men, such people can say their orientation is homosexual. If they choose to act on their orientation, and become sexually involved with some person(s) of the same gender, they can also say their *behavior* is homosexual. Once again, only behavior was a choice, and only after their orientation had become evident.

Many find that people of both genders arouse an innate sexual response within them, and realize that they're oriented toward possible sexual involvement with both men and women. Their choice of behavior thus includes responding to men or women or both. Their orientation is to both genders, so their orientation is bisexual—or "bi". But their behavior could be any of the three: if a bi-oriented woman chooses to become involved only with men, her behavior is heterosexual; if she chooses only women, her behavior is homosexual; if she chooses men and women, either concurrently or consecutively, her behavior is bi, or bisexual.

Thus, when a woman, for instance, is sincerely able to say, "I'm attracted to both women and men, and have been able to choose only men for my actual behavior," I interpret this to mean that while her behavior is heterosexual, her orientation is truly bisexual, and that in fact she is fulfilled choosing only one gender for actual behavior in the same way any person who remains monogamous in the face of coming across additional potential partners is fulfilled. One doesn't have to be interacting sexually with both genders at the same time to be bisexual in orientation or behavior.

A lesbian friend of mine addresses the question of "choice" most succinctly when she says, "I have no choice in my sexual orientation. My only choice is whether or not to be true to myself." In that statement lays the struggle many people find when they live a life where their orientation and behavior don't match. Most often it occurs when individuals recognize they have sexual attractions to (are oriented toward) persons of the same gender. Rather than accept that they're lesbian or gay and allow their behavior to match their same-gender orientation, they choose to go against their natural orientation and instead be sexual only with persons of the opposite gender (or to be celibate). They haven't changed their innate attraction to their own gender, they've simply chosen not to be true to it, and have chosen more socially acceptable heterosexual *behavior* instead.

If people on the outside misconstrue the gay or lesbian person's (incongruent) heterosexual behavior as an altering of their internal homosexual orientation, they're missing a vital distinction. Such persons may be living as heterosexual (or *presumed* heterosexual as in cases of celibacy), but they are *passing* as only/absolutely heterosexual because they are still living with all the internal reactions their body automatically provides during times of their true same-gender orientation attraction.

By attempting to block out or ignore those innate, unsolicited, magical sexual reactions within, such individuals can experience tremendous stress, especially when involved in behavior that doesn't match their true physical responses. The person's opposite-gender behavior may win praise and acceptance, but, inside, distress is a major complication. Relationships, emotions, health, and productivity can all suffer under the strain.

Thus, marriages entered into solely to try to follow society's myth that one's orientation is a choice are doomed, up front, either to failure or to much pain. Even if the two people do genuinely care for one another, even love one another, they're caught in a tormenting bind because one of the partners isn't being true to his or her basic nature, and the other often-unsuspecting partners all too often cannot figure out what is wrong, and may blame themselves for being unattractive and/or unfulfilling. By forcing people to pass for their safety and success, society sets up untold numbers of such broken homes and broken hearts.

Passing as heterosexual has numerous other societal prices beyond such marriages.

For example, even families of mutually-heterosexual persons can suffer as a result of the passing, as a result of the cultural silences that maintain the negative myths about homosexual people. For example, the untrue myth that homosexuals are automatically child molesters has a societal price, as declared by Anne in her interview:

> Our silence hurts children. By us not coming out and saying *it's not us* [not homosexuals per se], *but pedophiles*—adults who molest regardless of their sexual orientation—who are molesting the children in their homes, schools, etc., we helped keep that going, because no one tried to find who *was* harming our children.

In other words, with homosexuals labeled as *the* child molesters, heterosexual fathers, mothers, step-parents, grandparents, uncles, aunts, brothers, and cousins were free of scrutiny and of condemnation, despite a preponderance of research evidence that certifies the highest degree of danger is within a child's heterosexual circle of adults. Research that shows, for example, that "a child is 100 times more likely to be sexually abused by a heterosexual partner of a relative than by a gay adult" (Elovitz, 1995, in Jenny, FN56).

Every child molester should be caught, tried, sentenced and treated, regardless of sexual orientation. The stereotypes and scapegoating of homosexuals delays recognition that many *heterosexual* families are dangerous places for our children to be.

Heterosexuality is no guarantee of safe caregivers in other arenas, either. People known and trusted by children are the ones most able to abuse them. Religious leaders, counselors, teachers: what matters is whether or not they're *pedophiles*—attracted to children—not their same- or opposite-gender orientation (*Oregonian*, September 18, 1992.)

For those whose religious faith is an integral part of their family life, families all over the world felt deeply betrayed by the Catholic church scandal when, in the early 2000's, both men and women began to say priests had abused them when they were young. Despite all research showing child abuse to be an abuse of power, and that the majority of pedophiles are *hetero*sexual even when they abuse children the same gender as themselves *(Oregonian, 1992)*, the Catholic church's response was to refuse to ordain gay persons because some priests had abused some boys. As gays, lesbians, bisexuals, and their allies looked on in horror, the message this sent the world was that the Catholic church still equates pedophilia with homosexuality. It refused to follow the long-known majority research data that clearly states 'gay does not equal pedophile':

> The belief that homosexuals are particularly attracted to children is completely unsupported by our data. The child offenders who engaged in adult relationships as well, were heterosexuals. There were no homosexual adult oriented offenders in our samples who turned to children. (Groth and Birnbaum, 1978.)

The irony in the Catholic church's misguided "solution" of course is that their "remedy" ignored the fact that many girls were abused, too (or the Vatican couldn't quite make the consistent move to likewise refuse to ordain heterosexual priests because some had abused girls).

The church's unwillingness to realize that their remaining presumed-heterosexual priests will also still be a danger to both boys and girls *if they're pedophiles* was lost in their simplistic misguided attack on all gay priests. While the Catholic church may choose now to breathe a sigh of relief, all they've done is mistakenly let their guard down by focusing on the wrong solution, thus continuing to leave children of both genders at risk in church and church school settings.

Another price mutually-heterosexual couple families pay is in society's insistence that there are "right" and "wrong" sexual behaviors between consenting adults. In the United States, up until 2003, thirteen states still prohibited "sodomy" (any sex other than as-intended for procreation) between different- and/or and same-sex partners (Murray, *Washington Times*, 2002). Such legally punitive insistence that any consensual sexual act except traditional intercourse is morally wrong— not just between same-gender, but also between opposite-gender couples as well—is a determination out of step with actual practice among a tremendous proportion of society.

As Anne stated, "Society pays a price in sexual repression in general. If you repress consensual sex anywhere, it's repressed every-where." Even though U.S. sodomy laws were deemed unconstitutional in 2003, the long history of legislation and spoken norms upholding the view that the only "good" sex is sex intended or as-intended for procreation causes many people to experience guilt and/or anxiety as they request or experience other forms of sexual activity within their mutually heterosexual married or unmarried relationships. Others seek such sexually non-traditional involvement outside the relationship, once again leading to pain within their family.

Another reason bisexual and homosexual people often give for choosing to pass is that they're attempting to avoid heterosexual people's stereotypical fear that if a person is open about being lesbian, gay, or bi, that they are "recruiting" others to be like them. To para-phrase Wayne Pawlowski, a trainer for the national office of Planned Parenthood from his presentation "Understanding Sexuality in Our Society," he said

> Those [heterosexual] people must have a deep down belief that homosexuality is *so great* that if anyone breathes a word about it, everyone will defect to that side and the population will cease to reproduce itself and humanity will cease to exist!

This once again reflects the myth that sexual orientation is "a choice." If orientation were contagious or could be recruited, you can be absolutely certain that with at least ninety percent of the populace and almost all media, education, politics and religions promoting and recruiting non-stop for heterosexuality, if a choice could be made, *no one* would choose homosexuality. We don't speak up to recruit; we speak up to be honest. We pass and don't speak up for fear people might think we're recruiting. Where does it all end?

Family as a legal structure for adults and children

There's another entire realm of losses for families that is set in motion by society's insistence that the only acceptable families are opposite-gender. The costs can be high for those families who are directly affected. But once again, society also ends up paying additional prices it's created but is unaware of. Two legal constructs currently fail adults and children alike: marriage itself, and foster parent/adoption opportunities.

Marriage

Our culture has set up legal "civil marriage" as a structure designed to allow the government to bestow a multitude of legal benefits and responsibilities upon its participants. There is also "religious marriage" or "sacred marriage" too, of course, but a religious marriage, alone, does not grant the legal benefits offered by a civil marriage.

In the United States, for example, when a qualifying opposite-gender couple chooses to undergo a civil marriage to formalize their family relationship, suddenly approximately fourteen hundred federal and state legal and economic benefits and accompanying responsibilities are automatically theirs (Ontario Consultants on Religious Tolerance). These help the couple provide for one another, protect one another, and in many ways help stabilize their relationship.

With marriage for same-gender couples only starting to occur in some houses of worship and in a few scattered jurisdictions, few such benefits are available. For example, any state's civil marriage for same-sex couples, and "civil unions"[20] like Vermont's, only grant the several hundred state rights/benefits of marriage to the couples, but none of the over one thousand federal marriage benefits. Other locales like New York City grant a shorter list of marriage-equivalent benefits to registered same-sex couples. Without the full scope of benefits civil marriage provides, same-gender couples are less able to take care of one another and their children than opposite-gender married couples are.

For example, with legal civil marriage a couple can grant one another health insurance, hospital visitation, medical decision-making, retirement benefits, spousal privilege, child custody after death, housing eligibility, immigration eligibility, inheritance benefits, and more. Conversely, when a marriage ends in divorce, the legal system is set up to attempt to provide for both parties in their financial separation.

But when a couple is not able to marry, then the partners are less able to care for one another financially (while alive and after one's death). This leaves more people uninsured when an employee doesn't cover their partner (stressing the already overtaxed health care system) or can overstress a family budget to cover healthcare out-of-pocket. The extra financial or emotional stresses can be a detriment as stress can always be: affecting one's work performance, health, even commitment to the job. For example, it's not unusual for unmarried employees to seek a company that offers "domestic partner"[21] health benefits:

> a 1999 survey by the Society for Human Resource Management/ Commerce Clearing House found DP [Domestic Partner] benefits were the No. 1 recruitment incentive for executives and the third most effective recruitment incentive for managers and line workers. In that study, domestic partner benefits were viewed as more effective in enticing new hires than such perks as the option to telecommute, hiring bonuses, stock options and 401(k) plans. (Human Rights Campaign Foundation)

A reminder for those concerned that allowing same-sex marriage might conflict with their religious beliefs: no religious blessing is required for a civil marriage to be legal. Religions/denominations can already refuse to marry a couple if they so choose (as in Catholics denying remarriage to divorcees, or any faith requiring conversion of a betrothed before marriage). And on the other hand, a number of faiths now do allow same-gender couples to marry (for example the Unitarian Universalists, Metropolitan Community Church, United Church of Christ, and others).

Religious organizations are now and will continue to be free to perform or deny same-gender marriages—so what's at stake is the legal *civil* marriage opportunity, since it is what's denied all same-gender couples, regardless of religion, in the most countries today.

A slogan that's invariably raised by some religious persons who oppose gay marriage is "God made Adam and Eve, not Adam and Steve." I'm confident I'm not the only person who finds it to be ironically humorous. Because from my perspective, of course God created Adam and Steve. And Adam and Roberto and Booker and

Abdul and Francois and Toshiro and Alexei. And every man on the planet.

That God created men and women with their option to procreate isn't at question. That all humans were additionally created with the option to be consensually sexually satisfied with sensual/sexual behaviors that *don't* lead to pregnancy is the obvious missing link for the slogan-wavers.

I think everyone would agree it was optimal providential design to allow each and every human being to have a full sexual life without each and every sexual act automatically leading to pregnancy. Fortunately that's how we've been created. The Adam-Eve combination is one sexually fulfilling option that additionally allows occasional pregnancy. But Adam/Eve, Adam/Steve, and Anna/Eve are also all sexually fulfilling options that don't require or necessarily ever lead to pregnancy. In my view, God made every one of us in this way. No exceptions.

So to those who say we shouldn't marry because "marriage" is an institution designed for the procreation of children, I am not persuaded. Adam and Eve had children without benefit of marriage of course. But that aside: having children is not a prerequisite of marriage. If it were, sterile or older or childless-by-choice couples would be denied marriage. And perhaps more importantly: if marriage is for providing stable homes for children, then that argument alone should be the clincher for allowing us to marry:

> David Brodzinsky, Rutgers University psychology professor and clinical psychologist . . . said researchers estimate that up to 8 million children nationally are being raised by same-sex parents. . . . he also said states should not punish them by denying them benefits they could receive if their parents could marry. (Hosek, *Honolulu Star-Bulletin,* 2001)

If gay and lesbian civil marriages were allowed, then all those children could have two legal guardians instead of one, and could receive all the extra benefits dual parenthood entails: adoption, health insurance, guardianship, inheritance, etc.

And to those who say allowing same-gender marriage would "harm the institution of marriage," and insist the "sanctity of marriage" must be protected, I have to reflect on how sanctified (sacred) marriage is or is not, already, in this country.

In my family, for example, one of my sisters was married by a church, one by a justice of the peace, and another by a friend who has a license to perform civil (male/female) marriages. Thus only one of my sister's marriages was a religious (sacred/sanctified) marriage, even though all three were automatically given the full legal benefits of marriage. Since anti same-sex marriage opponents don't attack non-sanctified civil marriages like two of my sisters had—civil marriages, not religion-based—why should those anti-gay opponents feel compelled to attack other civil marriages such as same-sex marriages?

Marriage is only religiously sanctified if performed by a religious official; since already some citizens are free enter into non-religious legal civil marriages absent religion-given sanctity of marriage, why shouldn't others be able to, too?

I must add that while many people do sincerely fear for the state of the institution of marriage in our country, the anti-gay arguments about it fail to persuade me.

Already, about fifty percent of the marriages in the United States end in divorce. Marriage clearly is in trouble, but not because of people like me. Relationships are complex, and each and every one is on its own to try to navigate the many hurdles it will face as it tries to endure. Allowing another group of people to make the attempt won't hurt the institution. Rather, it will simply allow more who want to try to make a go of it that chance.

It might be of some (painful) help to remember that, historically, predictions of the destruction of marriage were also the norm when past changes were contemplated. For example,

> In the 1800's, both England and the United States began enacting laws designed to make marriage into a partnership of legally equal partners. As these changes were being considered, it was not unusual for opponents to predict catastrophe. When England was considering letting wives own property, The *Times of London* wrote that doing so would 'abolish families in the old sense' and 'break up society into men and women' creating 'discomfort, ill-feeling, and distrust where hitherto harmony and concord prevailed.' (Wald, 1999, p. 13)

And when legalizing interracial marriage was proposed in the United States, the furor again predicted catastrophe:

> Attorneys for the state of Tennessee argued that such [interracial] unions should be illegal because they are 'distasteful to our people

and unfit to produce the human race . . . .' The supreme court agreed, declaring [interracial] marriages would be 'a calamity full of the saddest and gloomiest portent to the generations that are to come after us.' (Zorn, *Chicago Tribune*, 1996)

It took until 1967 for interracial marriages to become legal throughout America. The *Chicago Tribune* quote, above, can parrot verbatim arguments used today against same-gender marriages with just the slightest change of focus. Some people today still are opposed to interracial marriage and some will always be opposed to same-gender marriage. But such oppositions don't mean the institution of marriage's success or failure hinges on whether or not either or both groups participate in it.

And of course, one of the many reasons the divorce rate is as high as it is is because of the societal pressures for people to pass as heterosexual, and passing has caused many gay and lesbian people to enter marriages that are doomed to failure because genuine physical attraction is not part of their marriage's possibility. I'm confident the divorce rate, and all its fall-out, would be lower if lesbian, gay, and bi couples could, instead, marry the person they most love and are attracted to.

On the more personal note, I fail to see how my marrying my partner of twenty-four years could possibly do any harm to anyone else's particular marriage. I've been in my committed monogamous relationship far longer than most of my co-workers. My domestic partner relationship has neither helped nor harmed any of my coworkers' traditional marriages, I'm sure. Nor have their married (or unmarried) relationships affected mine.

So why should my married coworkers be able to provide health and retirement benefits for their partners from day one of their marriages, while I still can't after all these years? The inequity is a constant thorn in my paw as a fairness issue. I look forward to the day when I can provide for my partner the same way my married coworkers do.

In the meantime, national polls show the majority feels same-gender marriage will happen throughout the U.S. this century (Stacey and Biblarz, *American Sociological Review*, 2001). The percentage supporting our marriage slowly increases with each passing year.

As the U.S. moves slowly in that direction, civil marriage for same-sex couples is already occurring elsewhere: Netherlands was the first in 2001, and Belgium legalized gay marriage in 2003. Two

Canadian provinces approved our marriages in 2003, and in so doing Canada became the first country where any lesbian and gay couple in the world could legally marry, since there's no residency requirement for civil marriage in Canada.

Legal "civil unions" like Vermont's (adopted in 2000) provide many marital benefits to couples who live in Vermont. Other countries have since granted civil unions too, such as Argentina, France, and Germany where civil unions offer some marriage rights for same-gender couples. The courts ruled for civil unions in Brazil in 2004; and in South Africa, where gay rights are part of the constitution since apartheid ended, in 2004 "activists are preparing litigation to have the common law definition of marriage extended to include same-sex couples" (The Associated Press, *San Francisco Chronicle*, March 4, 2004).

"Registered partnerships"[22] provide a scattering of marriage rights in a number of other countries such as Denmark (1989), Norway (1993), Greenland (1994), Sweden (1995), and Iceland (1996) (Lambda Legal Defense and Education Fund). In 2003 England approved "civil partnerships" granting same-gender couples many of the legal benefits of marriage.

"Domestic partnerships" grant some specific (limited) rights and responsibilities of marriage in a number of scattered U.S. jurisdictions. For example, in 2003 California approved a statewide domestic partner law that is scheduled to go into effect in 2005. If it withstands possible challenges—and if full civil marriage approval does not replace it—it would provide couples who register as domestic partner many but not all of the state's civil marriage rights and responsibilities (though again none of the over 1,000 legal federal marriage benefits).

The debate between granting same-sex couples civil unions/ domestic partnerships versus marriage is ongoing in the U.S. and elsewhere. For example, in 2003, the Massachusetts Supreme Court ruled it unconstitutional to deny same-gender couples the state-offered rights and responsibilities of civil marriage.

Ruling that 'separate is not equal,' the Massachusetts high court determined civil unions for same-sex couples did not grant equal treatment under the law, and put it to the legislature to implement full legal civil marriage for committed same-gender couples beginning in May of 2004.

In response, the legislature began efforts to try to amend its state constitution to ban civil marriage for same-sex couples and/or overturn any that are issued. Any such state constitutional amendment change could not go to the people for a vote until 2006 at the earliest, so Massachusetts' marriage laws may remain in flux for some time. But equal treatment by the state of Massachusetts for same-gender committed relationships was the court's stand.

Efforts along this line are sure to continue. A case in point: in California in February of 2004, in an act of civil disobedience, the City of San Francisco, with Mayor Gavin Newsom's full support, issued a civil marriage license to a lesbian couple: Phyllis Lyon, age 79, and Del Martin, age 83. The two women had been together for 51 years. Phyllis and Del are long-time pioneer activists in America's lesbian/gay civil rights movement.

During their civil marriage ceremony at City Hall, Phyllis and Del "stood facing each other and beamed when a city official pronounced them not husband and wife but 'spouses for life.'" (Dignan and Sanchez, *Washington Post*, February 13, 2004).

After theirs, within one month almost 4000 more civil marriages for same-sex couples were performed in San Francisco alone before a court injunction stopped the initial flow. Coast to coast, cities ranging from New Paltz, New York, to Portland, Oregon, quickly began issuing civil marriage licenses as well.

With the marriage of Phyllis Lyon and Del Martin, and all who followed, a threshold had been crossed. Same-gender couples had been married in a city's government-sanctioned ceremony in the U.S. and no one else's marriages had overnight gotten any better or worse as a result. As to what protection anyone's marriage could possibly need from the marriage of Phyllis and Del, that is a question which will be hashed over in the years ahead, to be sure. But on that February day, history was made and the sky did not fall.

> Lyon said she was sure the ceremonies would be challenged in court and was uncertain if they would be upheld. 'God knows what's going to happen,' she said.
>
> But she said that she and Martin, who will celebrate their 51st anniversary together on Valentine's Day, were proud—and amazed—by what they had been at last allowed to do.
>
> 'Things are happening that we never dreamed of,' Lyon said. (Dignan and Sanchez, *Washington Post*, February 13, 2004)

As this trend continues, more states and nations will surely adopt civil unions and/or same-sex marriage over time as opposition continues to fade. And opposition does fade, as evidenced in Vermont:

> The results of the 2002 election have all but made permanent Vermont's [2000] landmark civil unions law, with many supporters declaring that it has ceased to become a political issue. . . . 'I think civil union is now part of the life of Vermont,' said Democratic Rep. William Lippert. 'And there may always be a small group of individuals whose mission it will be to repeal civil union, but I think they are going to be a clearly distinct minority.' . . . . Attorney Beth Robinson, who argued the civil union case before the state Supreme Court, said the public has had a chance to weigh the dire threats critics attached to civil unions—the collapse of marriage and of civilization—and judged them to be hollow.
>
> 'In 2000, the opposition was able to play on people's fears of the unknown,' Robinson said. 'Between then and now, we've had two years of couples—both Vermont residents and out-of-staters coming to Vermont—joining in civil unions. It's quite clear that the parade of horribles predicted by opponents hasn't materialized.'
>
> 'It's made some families a little stronger and a little more secure, and it hasn't taken away from anybody else,' she said. (Data Lounge, Nov. 27, 2002)

The slow but steady groundswell of support for lesbian and gay marriage seems most assured due to the demographics of the growing acceptance. For example, in 2003 *USA Today* ran a story in which it reported two things: first that the American majority which opposes gay marriage is steadily declining (opposition dropped 13% between 1996 and 2003), and second that "a majority of young adults think such unions should be recognized by the law, according to a USA TODAY/CNN/Gallup Poll." In particular it reported that "61% of respondents ages 18-29 said homosexual marriages should be valid, while only 37% of those ages 30-49 felt the same." (Jones, 2003)

Younger people may be more supportive in part because they've been more apt, from an early age, to realize they personally know or know of people who are out (be it family or friends or famous celebrities). Older persons often didn't start becoming aware of the many lesbian, gay, and bisexual family and friends around them until much later in life, after people started coming out on a more regular basis. They may not have given much thought to the many issues involved until later adulthood.

But older people now, too, are beginning to think through the pros and cons of allowing their non-heterosexual coworkers and family and friends the possibility of the legal recognition and basic benefits that opposite-gender couples take for granted. As more and more same-gender couples they know do become married in accepting houses of worship, in countries like Canada, and in various states or jurisdictions, the concept will become increasingly familiar, and at some point should feel comfortable to a solid majority of citizens of all ages.

The obvious benefits of civil unions or marriage—couples who are better able to take care of one another and their children—help win more supporters over time. The resulting greater self-sufficiency and greater reciprocal legal responsibilities these couples are able to provide are sure to benefit not only those families, but everyone connected to them.

Despite increased support, with the heightened discussion of same-sex marriage and civil unions taking place in the U.S. and around the world it's probably not surprising that backlash can be harsh.

For example, in the U.S., in the face of Massachusetts' court ruling for equal treatment of same-gender couples (marriage or its equivalent), some U.S. Congress members began to again push banning same-gender marriage into the national political fray despite the fact that the national "Defense of Marriage Act" (DOMA) defining marriage as only between one man and one woman, and permitting states to refuse recognition of such unions if granted elsewhere, had already passed Congress back in 1996. In 2003, long-time anti-gay groups and individuals began calling on Congress to pass an anti-gay marriage constitutional amendment to, in their words, protect the sanctity of marriage, and to preserve marriage for the procreation of children, and other religious arguments. They claimed civil marriage for same-sex couples a threat to the institution of marriage and to the very fabric of society, and deemed it a central issue for upcoming elections.

A U.S. constitutional amendment would require a 2/3 vote of support in the House and Senate and passage in three quarters of the states. If passed, it would be the only amendment in the Constitution *denying* rights. Only alcohol-prohibiting Prohibition, which was quickly overturned, ever marked the Constitution similarly to deny rights in America.

It's hard to imagine another rights-denying amendment passing for a number of reasons, because Americans as a rule have been hesitant to change their freedom-founding document even to *give* rights.

For example, the Equal Rights Amendment (ERA), clarifying women's equality, wasn't able to make it into the Constitution despite federal and state laws guaranteeing equality regardless of gender. Women's equality became the law throughout the land nonetheless via those state and local laws, but not via a constitutional amendment.

The U.S. Constitution's durability is due in part to its success in providing durably broad guidelines to support the Declaration of Independence's promise that every citizen has an inalienable right to life, liberty and the pursuit of happiness. Voters have proven hesitant to use the Constitution to grant or deny rights when individual state and local laws, and federal laws, can suffice instead.

A *Washington Post* article touched on just a few of the reasons even many conservatives can't support amending the U.S. Constitution to deny marriage for same-gender couples:

> many leading conservatives oppose the amendment. George F. Will, for example, opposes it because he shares many conservatives' view that the Constitution should be amended only sparingly—and certainly not to resolve a contentious social issue on which public opinion is in flux. David Brooks opposes it because he wants gays to be included in societal norms of monogamy and fidelity. Former congressman Bob Barr opposes it because his own Defense of Marriage Act already prevents one state from forcing another state to recognize a same-sex marriage. House speaker Dennis J. Hastert has argued that DOMA needs to be tested in the courts before he is ready to press forward with an amendment. Conservative activist David Horowitz sees amending the Constitution as an opportunity for the radical left to try to amend the Constitution in turn, bringing the unifying founding document into disrepute. Others, such as Vice President Cheney, have said they believe that marriage should remain a state matter, as it always has been. (Sullivan, *Washington Post*, December 7, 2003).

Another reason many people of all political persuasions would oppose a constitutional Amendment is because of its proposed wording. Instead of only denying same-sex marriage, the early 2004 draft wording could also deny "the legal incidents" of traditional marriage. In other words, it would also deny civil unions or domestic partnerships. And some have argued that denying the legal incidents of marriage might even go further and strip same-gender couples of the scattering of hard-earned benefits they now have, here and there, such as health benefits in some companies, hospital visitation in some jurisdictions, etc.

Clearly a number of states, private industry, religious groups, and the younger people of America are moving slowly but steadily in the direction of increased support for equal treatment for their gay and lesbian and bisexual fellow citizens. This increased support aligns with the unfolding of the U.S. Constitution's original basic premises that all people are created equal under the law, with freedom from another person's religion.

Social change has lumbered forward since America's original Constitutional Convention, always in the face of harsh criticism, with each change to date granting more, not less, depth to the goal of liberty and justice for all. "The genius of federalism, after all, is that social change can be tried out in one state before it is enacted elsewhere" (Sullivan, *Washington Post*, December 7, 2003). The national debate on civil marriage and civil unions is in the midst of that state-by-state movement now, and I'm grateful I'm not alone in being confident a constitutional amendment is not the venue that will best serve our nation as a whole.

Foster parents/Adoption

We need not wait for legal marriage to amend another legal failing in this country: the foster parent and adoption laws that in many states bar same-gender couples, or acknowledged lesbian/gay individuals, from fostering or adopting children. Because of the untrue stereotypes about homosexuals being scary dangerous people, thousands upon thousands of willing adults are barred from being foster or adoptive parents. And as a result, children suffer.

Fortunately, every year more national organizations line up in support of our parental status:

> The nation's leading child welfare, psychological and children's health organizations also have issued policy or position statements declaring that a parent's sexual orientation is irrelevant to his or her ability to raise a child. Many also have condemned discrimination based on sexual orientation in adoption, custody and other parenting situations and called for equal rights for all parents and children. Further, several of these organizations also have issued statements

declaring that a parent's gender identity and/or physical appearance is irrelevant to his or her abilities as a parent.

Among the organizations that have done so: American Psychological Association, 1976. Child Welfare League of America, 1988. American Psychiatric Association, 1997. North American Council on Adoptable Children, 1998. American Academy of Pediatrics, 2002. American Psychoanalytic Assoc, 2002. American Academy of Family Physicians, 2002. (Human Rights Campaign Foundation, 2003)

The arguments made that children are automatically better off in a father-mother household can be heartfelt. But they don't match the majority research of the day. According to the American Academy of Pediatrics:

A growing body of scientific literature demonstrates that children who grow up with 1 or 2 gay and/or lesbian parents fare as well in emotional, cognitive, social, and sexual functioning as do children whose parents are heterosexual. Children's optimal development seems to be influenced more by the nature of the relationships and interactions within the family unit than by the particular structural form it takes. . . .

The AAP recommends that pediatricians become familiar with professional literature regarding gay and lesbian parents and their children; support the right of every child and family to the financial, psychological and legal security that results from having both parents legally recognized; and advocate for initiatives that establish permanency through co-parent or second-parent adoption for children of same-sex partners. (American Academy of Pediatrics, Technical Report, *Pediatrics*, 2002, pp. 341-344)

Fortunately, some states do allow same-gender parents fostering and adoption. But until all states do, many same-gender families are under pressures other families are not.

For example: the first 2003 New Year's Baby (front page on many newspapers) for the Washington DC area was born to a lesbian couple. They'd been together twelve years and had decided to have a child. In the best interests of their to-be-born child, they decided to move from Virginia to Maryland before the birth because the non-biological mother wished to adopt their baby, and Virginia wouldn't allow a second-parent adoption. The non-biological mother will commute to her job in Virginia. "We're not interested in any legal battles—that's why we moved," she said. "I really like living in Virginia. But it's more important to be a parent. " (Whoriskey, *Washington Post*, Jan 2, 2003).

If adoption were legal for same-gender parents in all states, the disruption of moving from a supportive network of friends and the stress of a commute would not have been part of this family's welcoming of their new family member.

When Rosie O'Donnell, popular TV talk show host, came out publicly as a lesbian in 2002, she did so in part so she could stop passing as straight and could better lobby for same-sex family adoption in Florida.

> 'I don't think America knows what a gay parent looks like: I am the gay parent,' the entertainer tells ABCNEWS' Diane Sawyer in her first in-depth interview about her sexuality.
>
> O'Donnell has three adopted children—Parker, 6, Chelsea, 4, and Blake, 2—and says she is in 'a committed, long-term life relationship' with her partner of about four years, Kelli Carpenter. She talked about her experiences as a gay parent publicly for the first time [with Diane Sawyer], hoping to bring attention to the issue of gay adoption and a Florida law that prevents gay couples from adopting.
>
> 'I wanted there to be a reason' to talk about her sexuality, she says. And when she learned about a Florida gay parenting case, she found that reason and has made it her cause.
>
> Steve Lofton and Roger Croteau are raising five HIV-positive children, three of whom are foster kids. The couple was able to adopt the other two in Oregon. The family was thrown into disarray when the state of Florida told them they had to give up one of their foster children, Bert, whom they have raised for 10 years. Lofton and Croteau would like to adopt Bert, but under Florida law they can't, because they are gay.
>
> When O'Donnell read about the Lofton-Croteau case, she thought about her adopted son Parker: 'My Lord, if somebody came to me now and said ... 'We're going to take him now because you're gay,' my world would collapse. I'm lucky to have adopted my children, not in the state that I live, Florida. I'm lucky, because otherwise I would be in danger of losing my children.' (ABC NEWS, Primetime, April 4, 2002)

Rosie had always been a champion for children's issues all her years as a talk show host; but by also coming out and being open as a lesbian, her decision to move beyond passing is sure to help make an immense difference in the lives of even more children. Moving beyond the need for passing is good for children. For parents. For families. For us all.

Loss of talent

Loss of talent is an incalculable price paid by society when so many people aren't or cannot easily be true to themselves.

It can take the form of the self-imposed under-employment many people choose in order to avoid the more extensive passing (passing as heterosexual, or passing with gender-conforming behavior) often required in higher-level jobs.

Or loss of talent can be caused by specific discrimination against people which bars them from jobs they do seek, thus disallowing them their chosen avenue of endeavor. And in the process disallowing the rest of us the benefit of their talent.

For example, in the aftermath of the 9/11 tragedy (the terrorist hijacking of passenger planes that destroyed the New York Twin Towers and a portion of the Pentagon), the Pentagon put out an urgent plea for recruits who could translate in Arabic languages. The response was slim, so it seemed more than incongruous when the *Washington Post* reported the following:

Ever since Sept. 11, 2001, government officials have been complaining that a shortage of employees proficient in Arabic has hampered the fight against terrorists.

The intelligence agencies have sought to recruit people with language skills so that documents and intercepts could be translated promptly. But in the military, at least, the desire to defeat al Qaeda has been preempted by an apparently more important priority: continuing the irrational discrimination against gay men and lesbians who would serve their country.

According to the Servicemembers Legal Defense Network, at least seven Arabic linguists—along with two Korean-language specialists and an expert in Mandarin Chinese—have been discharged from the services since the attacks last year solely because of their sexual orientation.

The gay ban, reflecting one of this country's last officially sanctioned forms of bigotry, stigmatizes patriotic Americans by excluding them from military life, often after intrusive witch hunts. By marginalizing those who wish to put useful talents at the service of their country, it also weakens America in its life-or-death struggle, which, as President Bush has repeatedly said, is profoundly different from previous wars. The military can't afford these days to waste human resources or turn away the energy of qualified men and women who wish to help. That is as true of linguists as it is of combat specialists. (*Washington Post*, Nov. 20, 2002)

Such blatant waste of talent should not have been an issue, because as long ago as the late 1980's the US Department of Defense commissioned a study to review its policy of barring homosexuals from the military. Unfortunately for us all, it was so surprised by the findings it rejected the report. Nevertheless, DOD's commissioned report found:

> The new report . . . executed by the Defense Personnel Security Research and Education Center concludes that the American military should reexamine its homophobic policy and consider ending anti-gay and lesbian discrimination. The unclassified study was made available by members of Congress, in particular Reps. Gerry Studds (D-Mass.) and Patricia Schroeder (D-Colo.).
>
> The study says homosexuals trying to join the military have stronger qualifications and fewer problems in their backgrounds than their heterosexual counterparts. 'These results appear to be in conflict with conceptions of homosexuals as unstable, maladjusted persons,' the Center's report concludes. The Center was established to analyze the kinds of people who could be trusted with secrets.
>
> The report compares the background records of 166 gays and lesbians who entered the military and were subsequently discharged because of their sexual preference with those of heterosexuals who were in the military. 'The preponderance of the evidence presented indicates that homosexuals show pre-service suitability-related adjustment that is as good or better than the average heterosexual's,' the report's author, Michael A. McDaniel concludes.
>
> The report looks at school conduct records, thinking skills, adjustment to military life and drug abuse. Homosexuals performed better in all except drug and alcohol abuse categories. (Diamond, *San Francisco Examiner*, October 29, 1989)

Drug and alcohol abuse

Drug and alcohol abuse, regardless of its provocation, poses another concern with a high societal price tag. Sexual minority persons certainly have no corner on the market for misuse of alcohol and drugs, but the percentage who do have a problem appears higher than within the overall population.

The frequent self-enforced isolation of passing, the stresses involved in creating or maintaining the illusion of heterosexuality, the self-contempt for constant "little white lies" or deceptions, fear of discrimination or violence, and the pain of reading and hearing constantly that "such people" are horrible/sick/perverts/should-be-shot/ etc./etc./etc., are among the many reasons that the numbing of feelings granted by drugs and alcohol becomes attractive to many bi, gay, transgender, and lesbian people.

Every person with a substance abuse problem affects not only their own mental and physical health, but also affects their family, friends, job, the safety of others on highways, and on and on. Lessening of the pressures that drive people to drug and alcohol use is a major aspect of overcoming such abuse.

Living a lie. A life of hiding. Alcohol and drugs can deaden the pain, but not end it. Each time a person courageously acts with integrity by choosing not to pass, she or he experiences a moment of liberation, a moment of integrity that is not unlike a high of its own. It is therefore probably no coincidence that there is a rapidly growing sobriety movement afoot among gay, lesbian, bisexual, and transgender people today.

As the work continues for expansion of equal rights regardless of sexual orientation and gender identification, and as more and more people are speaking up and spreading the word that they are *not* fearful strangers, more transgender, bisexual, lesbian, and gay people are beginning to feel better about themselves, and the challenge of sobriety becomes possible.

Society's loss of integrity

When society not only allows but promotes untrue myths about a sizeable portion of its citizens and allows to go unchecked violence and discrimination against those citizens when they break no laws other than to be different in their focus of same-gender attraction, gender identity, or gender-behavior, society does its citizens and itself damage.

We live in a nation where liberty and justice are supposed to be *for all*; but in this same nation "gay bashing" is a condoned sport and judges too often set light sentences on those who beat or even kill gay, bi, lesbian, and transgender (who are usually presumed by attackers to be gay) people (Bryant, 1989, p. 2).

With up to ten percent of the population being predominantly homosexual, and with approximately one in four families having a relative who is, everyone knows and cares about someone whose orientation is same-gender. *Society itself,* therefore, knows the stereotype used against its loved ones is a lie. Until the lie is conquered so that citizens no longer suffer needlessly, society daily fails to achieve the integrity it claims to aspire to.

Ripple effects: unexpectedly ever-present

The question, "What price does society pay for our passing?" was clearly an unexpected twist on the topic of passing for the people I interviewed. Almost without exception nothing came to mind right away. It took contemplating the price society perhaps paid for African-Americans passing as white, especially during the civil rights movement, but also today, for in depth discussion to take place around the question.

Said Barbara:

What price [that blacks passed]? An embarrassment. The majority culture so oppressed the minority that people thought passing was necessary. And, you can't say it just in the past tense! The price society pays for us passing is the same as any minority group: when some of your energy is devoted to being on stage, it takes energy away from more important things.

Anne:

Frankly, I think passing is not good. It's deadly because it's oppressive and dishonest, and harmful to the individual and society. Society doesn't grow that way. It's like talking to someone with their sunglasses on. You know how that feels.

Joan echoed the hesitancy felt perhaps by all when she at first focused on the belief that one's private life and one's silence about one's differences didn't present a price to society. But the look back at blacks' struggle for equal legal rights laws caused her to say, "Society's price for blacks choosing to pass as white? I suppose, in actuality, there was a delay in seeing that color didn't matter. The period of passing delayed recognition."

Gay, lesbian and bisexual African-Americans passing as heterosexual back during the civil rights movement of course caused its own delays—not in regard to equal rights on the basis of race, but as a missed opportunity to include equal rights on the basis of sexual orientation as part of the movement's goal of giving *everyone* the chance to be judged on the basis of their character.

For example, Bayard Rustin, "an eloquent and engaging [gay] African-American pacifist who was inspired by Gandhi, and in turn inspired Martin Luther King" (Leydon, *Reuters News*, 2003) only belatedly started to become well known in 2003, when the Public Broadcasting System aired a documentary of his life titled "Brother Outsider: The Life of Bayard Rustin."[23] The documentary revealed how Rustin was a vital part of the movement. He helped organize the 1956 Birmingham bus boycott and was *the* unpublicized organizer of the 1963 March on Washington where King's "I Have a Dream" speech made history.

Though Rustin was "openly and unashamedly gay" back then, the general public didn't hear about him or his visionary civil rights work for many decades, because: "to prevent his sexuality from becoming an issue that might undermine his noble causes, he remained scrupulously circumspect, maintaining a deliberately low profile while working in King's shadow." (Leydon, 2003)

Had Rustin not felt pressure and not been pressured to be an invisible force behind-the-scenes in the movement, what more might he have accomplished? And how many more people of every race might be more respectful of homosexuals—of every race—today?

By not addressing prominent people's relationships or sexuality, historians have, intentionally or unintentionally, left us all assuming everyone was heterosexual: a form of passing-by-editorial-omission.

But many key people in every country's history were in committed same-gender relationships. While we cannot know to what degree those long-past relationships were sexual, evidence often abounds of love that was undeniable.

How might history be different today if the general American public knew, for example, that Katharine Lee Bates, author of the song "America the Beautiful," was in a thirty-year relationship with Katharine Coman, a fellow Wellesley professor? A few years after Coman died, Bates wrote a friend, "So much of me died with Katharine Coman that I'm sometimes not quite sure whether I'm alive or not."

Presumed-heterosexuality, when corrected, can cause extreme discomfort to some as often a majority of the public initially prefers honored figures continue to pass, and not come out.

For example, when the U.S. Episcopal church ordained its first openly gay bishop in 2003, Bishop Gene Robinson, the reverberations rocked the Anglican faith in all corners of the globe. Heartfelt anguished debate within the church ensued, where supporters and opponents of the ordination struggled to maintain an interconnected church in the face of their different understandings of the Bible's teachings on homosexuality.

Ironically, the church was aware it had already had other gay bishops, such as Utah's Bishop Otis Charles. But since Charles didn't come out as gay until some years after retirement, the church hadn't yet had to deal with the issue directly.

"We've always had gay bishops," Robinson said. "The difference is I'm being honest about it." (Meade, 365Gay.com, 2003). His up-front honesty will surely give Bishop Robinson the internal freedom to offer himself 100% in the service of his church, instead of holding back or short-circuiting himself in the many ways closeted gay, bisexual, and lesbian religious leaders certainly felt/feel forced to do.

Who knows how many gifts and talents have been lost to the religious faiths everywhere due to the delay in letting everyone know not all of their beloved religious leaders were/are heterosexual.

Joan and I went on to discuss other forms of passing where other "delays" have taken place. One example was how President Roosevelt passed as able-bodied since his administration kept it secret that he used a wheelchair, and how that deception most certainly delayed recognition of people who experience disabilities as full, equal, and vital members of society.

Individuals' choices to pass for their success, or for the success of their causes, and society's support and actual insistence on such passing, clearly delays full acceptance of those viewed as "different." The price for bi, lesbian, and gay people passing as heterosexual, and for intersexual and transgender persons passing as always/only in one specific gender, must certainly be the same.

Reflections—

7. "a threshold had been crossed. Same-gender couples had been married in a city's government-sanctioned ceremony in the U.S. and no one else's marriages had overnight gotten any better or worse as a result. As to what protection anyone's marriage could possibly need from the marriage of Phyllis and Del, that is a question that will be hashed over in the years ahead, to be sure. But on that February day, history was made and the sky did not fall."

    a) If you are married, was your ceremony religiously sanctified (performed by a religious official), or was it a civil marriage (performed by a justice of the peace or other licensed marriage official)? Why?

    b) Regardless if you're married or not, do you think the sanctity of any particular person's religious marriage is lessened in any way by the civil (non-sanctified) marriages between men and women that are performed regularly in the country?

    c) Given that civil marriages are already granted without religious sanctity for men and women couples, do you think allowing civil marriages between same-sex couples constitutes a threat to other people's sanctity of marriage dire enough to amend the U.S. Constitution to deny it?

    d) Imagine if a constitutional amendment did pass to prohibit same-sex couples from marrying. Would your particular marriage be directly affected at all (improved? worsened?), or not? Do you imagine the marriages of your friends and family would be directly affected?

8. "Each time a person courageously acts with integrity by choosing not to pass, she or he experiences a moment of liberation, a moment of integrity that is not unlike a high of its own."

    a. Describe a time you spoke up for yourself, despite possible negative reactions from people around you. Why did you do it? How did it feel? Would you do it again?

b. Think of someone you admire for her or his courage. In what way(s) is s/he courageous?

c. Describe a time when you were courageous.

9. "Individuals' choices to pass for their success, or for the success of their causes, and society's support and actual insistence on such passing, clearly delays full acceptance of those viewed as 'different.'"

a. What examples of "passing" are you familiar with? (Passing as heterosexual, passing as white, passing as a person of color, passing as financially secure, passing as healthy, etc.)

b. What pressures do you think leads to such passing?

c. What ripple effects do you perceive from such passing?

Editorial for Reflection:

10. "long-time anti-gay groups and individuals began calling on Congress to pass an anti-gay marriage constitutional amendment . . . . They claimed civil marriage for same-sex couples a threat to the institution of marriage and to the very fabric of society, and deemed it a central issue for upcoming elections."

The following is a "My Turn" editorial I wrote for the *Juneau Empire* in 2003. The *Empire* titled it: "Marriage, biblical teachings not threatened by domestic partners."
What thoughts or feelings do you have upon reading it?

It's a Biblical disagreement, not a threat.

Everyone who credits the success of their marriage to the denial of same-sex marriages, please raise your hands.

Everyone who thinks banning same-sex marriages will save their troubled marriage or protect their marriage's future please raise your hands.

In my unscientific polls, no one seriously raises their hands. So what's up?

'Marriage' with its near 50 percent failure rate is, of course, in trouble. But it's with no help or harm from committed gay and lesbian relationships.

So to suggest a U.S. Constitutional amendment denying same-sex marriage would make any difference at all to opposite-sex marriages just doesn't match reality.

What does match reality is that while it won't improve man-woman marriages, it would hurt same-sex couples and their children in innumerable ways.

Why? Because that no-marriage amendment would also bar civil unions like Vermont's and it wouldn't allow marriage-like benefits at all for same-sex couples.

Hospital visitation, inheritance, decision-making in times of accident or illness: these and over a thousand more rights and benefits are automatic in marriage. Barring them all from all same-sex couples is untenable.

My thanks to Ellie Sica, high school student, for saying it bothers her that much of the rhetoric against same-sex couples is mean. Much of it is. She recognizes the sting, asking if married people would want angry callers comparing their spouse to a dog? But much worse attacks are out there, of course. I've been told homosexuals deserve to be stoned to death because the Bible says so.

Thankfully, most people aren't so literal regarding the Bible's few anti-gay verses. What's ironic is that those who do attribute their anti-gay statements to scripture don't see they radiate Biblical noncompliance themselves.

When they stand before me unabashedly breaking Biblical prohibitions, there's just no way I can take them seriously on the few verses they use against homosexuals.

Why don't they condemn the following instead: the Bible bars women from braiding their hair, wearing pearls or gold (goodbye wedding rings), and wearing slacks. It bars men from shaving their sideburns. It bars tattoos. It bars men from being taught by women. Eating pork or shellfish, like homosexuality, is an abomination (imagine the Alaska seafood industry if that one prevailed).

The Bible also says loaning money at interest (usury) is deserving of death. But can you imagine capitalism without it? Everyone with a credit card or car loan is ignoring Biblical prohibitions by choosing to practice it.

So to all who say a Constitutional amendment against same-sex marriage is a Biblical necessity, I say, how about one to ban interest loans first? Imagine the reduction of personal and national debt!

Or there's Deuteronomy, saying men are not to serve in the army for a year after marrying. That's another Constitutional amendment I'm surprised no one's jumping on.

Bible interpretations clearly change over time. Not the words, but our understanding of them. History is clear: in every era many devout believers shift their understanding.

Such a shift is underway today. Some people still condemn homosexuality with religious fervor. But since they do so while visibly breaking many Biblical taboos themselves, I believe at some level they must appreciate how the rest of us can't accept their case as any kind of Biblical absolute.

Some faiths already support gay marriage (United Church of Christ, Unitarians, etc). Others don't. So as a religious decision, it seems obvious to say 'let each church decide.'

As to civil marriages, since states are also free to disagree, I likewise say 'let each state decide.'

Amending the U.S. Constitution for a few passages some people still choose to take literally, while not amending it for all the others—that's not Biblical consistency. It's selective bias: an attempt to enshrine some people's current religious views into the one document central to American equal freedom and pursuit of happiness that is supposed to give rights, not take them away. Fortunately, not all religious people agree, so why should the Constitution take a stand?

So, now, I have to ask: will everyone living in full accordance with just the few Bible prohibitions I listed above, please raise your hands?

How many hands do you see?

(Boesser, Sara, *Juneau Empire*, December 17, 2003)

8. How do the Societal Pressures that Demand Passing Hurt Everyone?

By creating a social environment where no one dares speak of let alone acknowledge non-heterosexual thoughts, or gender nonconformist thoughts, without facing painful if not potentially life-threatening consequences, what does society itself lose out on? What price does the entire fabric of society pay when passing as heterosexual, and as traditionally male/female, is a mandatory "norm"?

Whom does passing serve?

For now we see in a mirror dimly, but then face to face.
Now I know in part; then I shall understand fully,
even as I am understood. ~ *I Corinthians 13-12*

After living lifetimes of internalized oppression in which people have chosen to pass because they truly believed it "best for everyone," it feels almost treasonous to theorize on the possibility that passing is, in actuality, *bad for everyone*. It's a concept that shakes the foundations of reality for not just the people who knowingly suffer from anti-gay/lesbian/bi/trans/inter oppression, but also for heterosexuals and anyone chafing under traditional gender role restrictions as well.

So the question to ponder, the challenge for people of every sexual orientation and every gender identity experience, is: What if the overall extensive harm caused by passing means, in the big-picture cultural overview, that passing actually serves no one at all?

What if *not passing* is best for everyone?

Personal impact over a lifespan:
broader scope than expected

Far more people are affected on a personal level by society's oppressive judgment of homosexuals than just those who consider themselves lesbian, bisexual, or gay. While the original Kinsey reports of the
1940's and '50's identified that approximately ten percent of the
population is homosexual (Kinsey, 1948, p. 651 / 1953, pp. 472-474),
that number is in fact misleadingly small as a reflection of who feels
targeted by society's intolerance of homosexuals.

In the updated 1990 publication, *The Kinsey Institute New Report
on Sex*, the question is once again posed: "What percentage of the U.S.
population is homosexual?" The answer elaborates on Alfred Kinsey's
original ten percent findings:

> It depends on how you define 'homosexual.' It helps to distinguish
> between a person's sexual orientation label (how you identify your-
> self—as heterosexual or homosexual), and his or her actual behavior
> (who you had sex with this week, last year, ten years ago). For
> example, research indicates that between 62 and 79 percent of men
> who label themselves homosexual have had sex with women . . . and
> that 74 to 81 percent of lesbian women have had at least one sexual
> encounter with a man. . . . Thus the label a person chooses may not
> accurately describe or predict all sex behaviors and partners across a
> lifespan.
>
> *Approximately one-third of all males* are thought to have had at
> least one same-sex experience leading to orgasm since puberty. . . .
> Only about 4 percent of men were exclusively homosexual
> throughout their entire lives.
>
> Among US females, Kinsey found that around *half of college-
> educated women* and approximately *twenty percent of non-college-
> educated women* had at least one same-sex erotic contact past
> puberty; only 2 or 3 percent of these women were exclusively
> homosexual their entire lives. [italics added for *Silent Lives*]
> (Reinisch with Beasley, 1990, pp. 139-140, 142)

Thus it's very clear that far more people than the usually
contemplated ten percent have had some personal experience placing
them in the realm of homosexual behavior. With approximately one-
third of men and between twenty and fifty percent of women having
been sexually intimate with a person of the same gender at some time in

their lives, society's heavy judgment and intolerance of same-sex intimacy burdens far many more people than is acknowledged.

Even for those who only had one such experience, their resulting feelings—be they positive ones of love, and/or negative ones such as guilt or fear of later exposure—most often cause them to also become silent and to pass as always/only heterosexual for fear of suffering the ongoing attacks and disdain leveled at persons who are actually involved in same-gender relationships in present time.

Such inner turmoil is also prevalent from several other perspectives. Fantasy is one. The 1990 Kinsey report states researchers discovered that "one of the most common fantasies among heterosexuals is having sex with a same-sex partner" (Reinisch with Beasley, 1990, p. 140). For heterosexuals whose real-life sexual partners are only of the opposite gender, these recurrent same-gender dreams or fantasies can present a confusion and often an anxiety they're unable to work through because they keep silent for fear of being attacked for "incorrect" thoughts. Many feel guilt or shame, often for religious reasons, fearing there's something wrong with them, and the resulting stress in their lives can affect not only them, but also their relationship with their heterosexual partner or spouse. By keeping silent and passing as a person who has *only* heterosexual thoughts, the individual is unable to find relief from their inner discord because she or he doesn't discover the information that it's perfectly normal for fantasy behavior and actual behavior to be very different.

The concern over fantasies not matching behavior works both ways. Some people who consider themselves homosexual also have dreams of sexual encounters with a person of the opposite gender. They may not, in fact, ever feel drawn to seek out an opposite-gender partner, but many wonder why such incongruous dreams enter their sleep. They then also face confusion and stress, and are also often unwilling to talk of their concern for fear their lesbian and gay friends or partners might challenge them for having inappropriate thoughts.

Young people are especially susceptible to confusion about their sexuality. In puberty, especially when the young person does not have much, if any, actual sexual behavior, fantasies are paramount. When an adolescent experiences fantasies of same-gender sexual partners, he/she may not dare to discuss them with anyone. In the 1990 Kinsey report, a boy writes to the Institute:

> I'm in my late teens and I think I might be gay (or bisexual). I would rather not live if I have to live that lifestyle. I know it's OK for some

but not for me. . . . I've heard of a drug that disrupts all sexual desire. That might be my last hope. (Reinisch with Beasley, 1990, p. 142)

The response from the Kinsey Institute informs the teenager that no drug is known to influence sexual orientation, then goes on to say:

It's important to remember that sexual feelings aroused by a person of the same sex, fantasizing about same-sex activities, or even having sex with another male are not accurate predictors of your adult sexual orientation. In fact, approximately one out of every three men has had at least one same-sex experience since puberty. (ibid., p. 142)

As readers, we'll never know if the boy was in fact to live as a homosexual, or bisexual, or if he was actually to live as a heterosexual and was only having the fantasy of same-gender behavior that is common to so many heterosexuals. However, he zeros in on a critical issue: the fact that he well might not live at all because he might choose to take his life rather than face life as a homosexual. Government research reports:

A majority of [homosexuals'] suicide attempts take place in their youth. . . . Gay males were 6 times more likely to make an attempt than heterosexual males. Lesbians were more than twice as likely to try committing suicide than the heterosexual women in the study. A majority of the suicide attempts by homosexuals took place at age 20 or younger with nearly one-third occurring before age 17. (Gibson, 1989, p. 3-111)

Suicide is too often the solution youth turn to not only when they are lesbian, bi, or gay, but also when they fear they might be. This danger is unwittingly caused by the tremendous number of adults who pass as having *always* been *only* heterosexual in their thoughts and behavior, despite their actual experience as revealed by the 1990 Kinsey report.

Since the adults fear they'll be considered abnormal if they speak of their reality, most are rigidly silent, allowing a massive silence to exist, the commonality of experience unknown. Society as a whole and youth in particular remain unaware of the fully normal range of human sexual fantasies and experiences over the course of a lifetime.

Youth who cannot survive the rejection and mistreatment of being attacked for being (or considered) gay or lesbian or bi, or who have exhausted their efforts to pass as heterosexual and do not wish to face adverse results of coming out, or who just do not accept that they are—or might be—homosexual, imagine they're better off dead than alive. And, importantly, they believe this is best not just for themselves but for others, that is, "for society" as a whole. Suicide attempts result. And their death can trigger the death of others. Families and friends suffer. Each and every one's passing has failed in its goal of protecting each and every one.

Gender role restrictions

Avoiding being denounced for unacceptable sexual orientation is, perhaps surprisingly to some, actually at the very heart of our culture's socialization process.

While we all learned the societal rules defining what good little girls and good little boys did and didn't do, few of us envisioned the personal losses such rigid gender definitions imposed. No one told us that as long as there are appropriate interests and activities for girls that differ from those for boys, no one human being could ever be totally free to explore and develop fully all of her or his genuine innate potential and talents.

How many girls remember being good at, say, math in early grades, before they realized it was "not cool"? Maybe the message was direct, said to them by a teacher or a friend. Or, maybe it was subtle, and they just received much more adult praise for their successes in classes such as English or drama. The result: involvement with math fell away. Boy counterparts, on the other hand, who found joy in, say, poetry, received the opposite feedback, finding that peers and adults alike either discounted the poetry or simply didn't give it any praise to the point that it vanished from the youth's list of valued interests.

One (heterosexual) friend, Janis, reflected back to her high school days where initially she had been "blissfully smart." A late bloomer sexually, she reflects on how gender role expectations exploded her reality when puberty arrived:

> I remember when I started catching on that being so smart was crippling me socially. And it was like one day to another. I remember one day I was in science class raising my hand and suddenly realizing, 'This is not cool.' I literally overnight went from brilliant in science and math to on purpose being a bumble. A teacher noticed and got angry, and yelled that he knew I knew the answers, and that it

was sexual what I was doing [that is, playing down her intelligence to become more attractive to boys]. He was right, of course, but he couldn't offer me a social life. I realized I wasn't going to get anywhere [with boys] if I didn't start to act a little more stupid. I had to become soft and silly and stupid. And the real irony of it is I didn't do that well—I did it, but it never paid off. It's a bad system altogether. By the time I left home, by the time I was a senior, I took the bulk of me and locked it up somewhere, because it didn't fit; I didn't fit. I locked my self away to pass as a correct female.

Sometimes society's expectations for gender roles affect people in the very opposite way, causing individuals to reject certain actions or careers because those careers *are* so expected of them. Take Beatrice, for instance. An at-home, heterosexual married mother with two young children, she remembers,

What's obvious now to me is that I was interested in teaching, because I really enjoyed being with young children. But to me, that was always a 'woman's career.' It was like all women did that, so I wasn't going to do that. My dad was a dentist; he encouraged me to be a dental hygienist; he never encouraged me to be a dentist. So forget it. Women do that—forget it. Now I think, maybe I could've done them, getting rid of the stereotypes. Instead of being who I was, I always rebelled against it, too, took a rebellious stand.

What did each of us give up, fail to explore, or forget about simply because of the male or female gender role we embodied? What special talents were lost to society? What inventions failed to materialize, what diseases might have been conquered, what leadership went undeveloped, what works of art or music went uncreated?

It takes tremendous courage for any person to attempt to be true to themselves when that inner truth includes activities and interests outside traditional narrow gender roles.

Transgender people of course are the most visible challenge to society's rigid gender role behavior requirements, since transgender people know from earliest childhood that gender roll expectations do not fit for them. But unknown to society, our culture's gender restrictions have shortchanged *everyone* in the range of options regarding who and what each person could be. If people weren't afraid of being treated as not fully-male or as not fully-female, they'd never succumb to such abandonment of self.

And what does it mean, culturally, to be outside the "normal" gender roles, to be viewed as not fully-male or not fully-female? Fully male, fully female, culturally, means "normally" sexual: heterosexual. Conversely, society automatically labels people outside the traditional gender roles as being sexually abnormal. And what is sexually "abnormal"? Homosexual.

If society were not so insistent upon maintaining the negative stereotypes about lesbian and gay people, then straying from traditional gender role behavior would not be viewed so harshly, and people wouldn't suffer such mistreatment when they stray from expected "male" or "female" interests and occupations.

But mistreatment is society's method for keeping people in line, and it ranges from passive withdrawal of support for gender-inappropriate behavior to the extremes of gay- and trans-bashing where people who are or appear to be gay or transgendered are threatened or beaten or killed. Mistreatment can also extend to self-inflicted harm, including suicide.

In an article titled "Jerry's Choice: Why Are Our Children Killing Themselves?" the author points out that:

> though young women are more than three times as likely to attempt self-annihilation as young men, males are so much likelier to accomplish it that the disparity is one of the major puzzles of the field. . . . 'Why are males using more deadly means?' asks Dr. Carol Huffine, research director at the California School of Professional Psychology in Alameda, California. . . . One of the critical factors may be society's more rigid expectations for men . . . 'The pressure to conform is greater, its costs in self-esteem higher if they don't. It's not terrible if a girl is called tomboy—women brag about it as adults. But it's *terrible* if a boy is called a sissy.' (Wartik, 1991, p. 74)

"Sissy." Not fully-male. The ultimate attack: gay.

Boys, living within the more traditionally violent of the gender roles, suffer more violence even at their own hands. And boys who are unable to survive the intimidation of being called gay, regardless of whether they actually are or not, suffer acutely when their identity is attacked in that way. A violent death can be one last attempt for many of them to conform, to pass, to act within the expected gender role for "real men."

It's risky to act outside the narrow confines of traditional gender roles. The message is clear: step out too far and the bottom-line attack will be to be called "lesbian" or "gay." One of the tools used to discredit the women's rights movement, for instance, has been automatically to label women who take jobs outside "traditional women's work" as lesbian, simply as a way to keep *all* women in line. Avoiding the label and its persecution costs the overall workforce when women do then choose to stay in line, often wasting talents that could benefit society as a whole.

Another way gender expectations harm the overall optimal use of the workforce is the hidden element of gender-role expectations in employment decision making.

It's not a rare occurrence for people to not be hired or not be promoted simply because their behavior is outside traditional gender expectations. This means that not only homosexual and transgendered individuals can lose job opportunities if they exhibit a broader range of gender behavior than is the expected "norm," but that many heterosexual persons, too, also receive negative reactions and suffer lower job possibilities if they are *suspected* of being gay or lesbian if they dare to exhibit behavior outside narrow expectations. Lesbian, bi, trans, and gay persons are conscious of this employment screening for non-heterosexual behavior. If more heterosexuals consciously realized how they, too, face its unforgiving eye, they'd understand that everyone loses when employment decisions are made, consciously or unconsciously, on qualities so totally unrelated to the job-related merits and skills the applicant is actually offering to the job.

Thus, while sexual minority people know they must pass as heterosexual for their safety, their heterosexual majority counterparts must pass too, and must pay whatever price they perceive as necessary to be viewed as fully heterosexual and beyond reproach.

Cooper Thompson, author of the essay "On Being Heterosexual in a Homophobic World," published in the book *Homophobia: How We All Pay the Price* (Blumenfeld, 1992), wrote of the blanket of potential danger unchecked homophobia perpetuates:

> After a young gay man was murdered in Bangor, Maine, several years ago, I was asked to come and work with public school teachers on issues of homophobia. As I walked through the town, I sensed *every* man in Bangor must adjust his behavior; *any* man was vulnerable to attack if the attackers thought he were gay. About a year later, I was walking in Harvard Square in Cambridge (a place with a reputation for personal freedom) and was verbally assaulted

for having my arm around another man (I was helping him through a difficult period in his life). (119, p. 241)

And the very real danger doesn't stop at verbal harassment:

Anyone who doesn't meet expectations for a 'real man' or a 'real woman' can become a target, from a successful professional like Anne Hopkins in the Supreme Court's Hopkins v. Price Waterhouse case, who was fired for being 'too aggressive,' to African-American bus-driver Willie Houston, who was killed while celebrating his engagement when a man became enraged at seeing him holding a blind friend on one arm and his fiancé's purse on the other. (GenderPac, 2003)

What societal influence allows anti-gay/anti-lesbian attacks to be so prevalent? In the 1990 Kinsey report, the question was posed, "What are the reasons for anti-gay attitudes in our society?" An excerpt from the answer is revealing:

The causes of *homophobia* (fear, dislike, or hatred of homosexuals) are as unclear as the causes of many other prejudices. But there are studies which have compiled a long list of traits associated with the issue.
    Those with anti-homosexual views often think they do not personally know any homosexuals; have peers who display negative attitudes toward homosexuals; are less educated; attend church more frequently; have rigid concepts about appropriate sex roles; and are highly authoritarian. People like this are often vocal in their opposition to homosexuals as a way of announcing to the world that they are most definitely heterosexual, want to be treated like one, and expect everyone around them to be heterosexual also. (Reinisch with Beasley, 1990, pp. 147-8)

The paraphrased Shakespearian line, 'I think thee dost protest too much' is a concept that comes to the mind of many lesbian, gay, and bisexual people when they hear stridently anti-homosexual people, especially people in the public eye such as politicians and political/religious leaders, berating homosexuals.

This is not to say we necessarily suspect them of being homosexual at some time in their lives, though that thought may occur to us. But many of us perceive that such antagonists experience some personal pain around the subject, or else they'd be more apt to be among the non-threatened, non-threatening people who either "live and let live" or who sincerely "do unto others as they'd have done unto them." At the base of such tirades against homosexuals is quite probably some distant, possibly unremembered, attack of some sort against the antagonist personally. Those past attacks knowingly or unknowingly cause them to want to keep as much distance from any additional attacks as humanly possible. "Prejudice reduction theory" is an explanation for this interpretation of their behavior (National Coalition Building Institute, NCBI).[24]

Current prejudice reduction theory points out that people tend to hurt others in areas in which they themselves have been personally hurt, and will continue to do so until they're able to face and heal the old hurts they suffered. Since so many ingrained hurts occurred in childhood, we're all often unaware of the hurts that motivate us later in life, or are unaware of the way(s) in which they motivate prejudice within us.

And no one can honestly say she or he is totally free from prejudice. For a seemingly but not so innocuous example, I was born in the South, and lived there for four years followed by four years in Texas. When I moved to Alaska in the second grade, (southern/Texan drawl in full swing) my first acquaintance, soon to become my best friend, stamped her foot and said, "I won't play with you if you don't stop talking funny." Shocked, and not wanting to be lonely, I quickly learned to talk northwestern, and remembered the incident only with humor through the next three decades of recounting it.

It wasn't until my late thirties that I fully faced the fact that I had a distrust and lack of respect for heavy drawls—a definite prejudice—that was causing me to distance myself from people who'd had absolutely nothing to do with that childhood disruption.

Though I loved, and love today, the friend who made the statement, at some deep level it had upset my sense of self. It had hurt. As an adult, I was actually suffering that old hurt over and over again each time I withdrew from anyone who had a heavy Southern accent. In an effort to distance myself from feeling that old hurt, I distanced myself from people I associated with it.

To overcome that unnecessary prejudice I had to, in effect, go back to that shocked child within myself, admit the incident had hurt, and, by examining it from my more understanding adult perspective, find an internal sense of peace with what I had experienced so long ago. The end result is that now I recognize when I start to back away from the accent, catch myself and gently remind myself that the accent causes no harm to the adult me. As a result of this intentional re-visioning of my earlier prejudice, I often find myself today actually *more* attentive to a deep Southern accent than to some other speech patterns I hear.

I believe that part of the fearful response people have to "those homosexuals" is this same principle in action. The more a child was teased or bullied or attacked for being not strong enough, not masculine enough, not feminine enough, the more their core sense of self was potentially hurt. If their pain was great enough, severe anti-gay/lesbian behavior might feel like their best (unconscious) self-protective mode of safety as adults. But unfortunately, they're reliving, however unconsciously, their own experiences of attack each time they attack someone else. Thus their abusive behavior never gives them peace. It perpetuates the turmoil not just in society, but within themselves as well.

If, on the other hand, society's rigid gender roles were relaxed so that any person could be free to safely examine his or her full potential with no fear of being attacked in the process, such painful childhood experiences could cease to happen. Each talent, regardless of a person's gender, would be valued, and the motto "be all you can be" would take on a whole new meaning.

In other words, remove the bottom line attack—an accusation of homosexuality and the accompanying disastrous treatment promised to anyone bearing that label—and *all* personal lives could more freely flourish. Society itself would benefit immeasurably from the bounty of talent it would certainly inherit.

Questions for Reflection—

11. "Avoiding being denounced for unacceptable sexual orientation is, perhaps surprisingly to some, actually at the very heart of our culture's socialization process."

    a. Were you ever teased or ridiculed for being "sissy" or "tomboy"? Attacked?

    b. Do you remember other children who were?

    c. Do you think awareness of this danger either consciously or unconsciously affected what you did, what you wore, or who your friends were?

    d. What kinds of things did you do to "prove" you were a "real boy" or a "real girl"?

    e. If you're female, were you ever teased or ridiculed for being "too feminine"? If you're male, were you ever teased or ridiculed for being "too male"? How did it feel?

12. "What did each of us give up, fail to explore, or forget about simply because of the male or female gender role we embodied? . . . Unknown to society, our culture's gender restrictions have short-changed *everyone* in the range of options of who and what each person could be. If people were not afraid of being treated as not fully-male, or as not fully-female, they'd never succumb to such abandonment of self."

    a. What were your favorite hobbies or classes in the third or forth grade? Ninth? Today?

    b. Were you ever pressured to give up an interest or hobby? To take one on?

    c. Did anyone ever attack you verbally or physically for doing something outside traditional gender roles? How did you respond?

d. Did friends or family ever simply ignore any interests of yours? Hobbies?

e. Did you ever intentionally avoid a job or activity because it either *was* expected of you as a woman/man; or because men/women *don't* traditionally do that sort of thing? Do you remember people you knew who experienced any of these situations?

f. Are there any hobbies or interests you keep secret today because others might find them (and thus, you) outside traditional gender interests?

13. "Thus, while sexual minority people know they must pass as heterosexual for their safety, their heterosexual majority counterparts must pass too, and must pay whatever price they perceive as necessary to be viewed as fully heterosexual and beyond reproach."

a. To be perceived as fully heterosexual, what stereotypical things must you: talk about? read? watch? attend? buy? wear? drive? own? eat/drink/smoke? other?

b. Where did you get these stereotypic messages?

Reflections—Guided exercise:
Arbitrary Safety Zones

14. "'After a young gay man was murdered in Bangor, Maine, several years ago, I was asked to come and work with public school teachers on issues of homophobia. As I walked through the town, I sensed *every* man in Bangor must adjust his behavior; *any* man was vulnerable to attack if the attackers thought he were gay. About a year later, I was walking in Harvard Square in Cambridge (a place with a reputation for personal freedom) and was verbally assaulted for having my arm around another man (I was helping him through a difficult period in his life). (Thompson, 1992, p. 241)'"

Arbitrary Safety Zones

Here's a challenging exercise. It can be done solo, in your imagination. Or, if people in a group are willing to try something guaranteed to bring up nervous comments and laughter, and not a small amount of perspiration, it can be an interesting group experience.

Before you start, relax, lighten up. Feel free to read it through first before volunteering as it can be quite a challenge to one's internalized homophobia to do this.

Remember: we all first learned our reactions somewhere such a long, long time ago.

Two *volunteer* men participants stand up side by side in front of the group (or two women can volunteer for the same exercise; but remember it's apt to be much harder for men). In all the scenarios below imagine you're in a public setting surrounded by many people—most of whom you don't know.

[Note: responses can be spoken aloud, or written down, or everyone can just process their own reactions silently to themselves while a moderator explains what's happening at each stage of the process.]

First: the two volunteers hold one another's hand, right in left, standing side-by-side both facing forward toward the audience, which is told you're in a sports huddle.
    Audience: describe your comfort level? Why?
    Participants: your comfort level? Why?

Second: continue to hold hands side-by-side facing forward, this time as if a picket line, blocking others' passage.
    Audience: describe your comfort level? Why?
    Participants: your comfort level? Why?

Third: continue to hold hands side-by-side facing forward, this time as if at prayer.
    Audience: describe your comfort level? Why?
    Participants: your comfort level? Why?

Fourth: continue holding hands side-by-side facing forward with the audience told there's no clue why you're doing so.
    Audience: describe your comfort level? Why?
    Participants: your comfort level? Why?

Fifth: Continue holding hands as before, for no apparent reason, but move closer together.
    Audience: describe your comfort level? Why?
    Participants: your comfort level? Why?

Sixth: participants continue holding one another's hand as before, but this time turn and face each other, with a friendly look on your faces.
    Audience: describe your comfort level? Why?
    Participants: your comfort level? Why?

Seventh: participants shake hands, take a bow to the audience, and return to your seats.

Lastly: applaud the volunteers!

The title of the previous exercise is "Arbitrary Safety Zones." In each setting the action of the participants was the same: holding one another's hand. But reactions to that one action can vary tremendously, arbitrarily: from sports-acclaim and religious virtue to worthy-of-death (as in when presumed-gay men are killed for "flaunting their sexuality that way" in public).

During the exercise, did any of your reactions or internal dialogue surprise you? Did you go through any particular checklist in your mind for each scenario? Why and where do you think you learned or were taught that checklist/reaction? How comfortable would you be crossing the arbitrary safety zones of the culture when it comes to hand-holding in public?

For another version, two women can volunteer the same exercise. How are people's reactions the same? Different? Why do you think this is? And, how arbitrary is it that reactions to women might be different than to men?

Inhibiting protection of children and the healing of adults

There is another price of passing that our children must bear and carry unhealed into adulthood. It's the pain and terror of their unreported childhood sexual abuse.

While society is slowly, finally, beginning to acknowledge and respond to the fact that many girls suffer from sexual abuse at the hands of pedophiles (adults who sexually abuse children), society is far slower to address the abuse suffered by boys. Homophobia—fear, dislike, and hatred of homosexuals and homosexuality—is a major compounding element of this denial of abuse against boy children. Each boy that doesn't receive treatment and healing for his abuse runs an increased risk of also becoming an abuser as an adult.[25] So future generations of girls and boys alike are endangered by the silences homophobia imposes on men who as boys suffered sexual assault by a man.

Current estimates show that as many as one in four girls and one in ten boys have been sexually abused before the age of consent (Whealin, 2002); and many researchers believe these figures are too conservative. The large majority of the reported cases of abuse against both girls and boys is abuse by fathers, step-fathers, or other self-identified heterosexual men known to the victim (Elovitz, in Jenny, FN56).

Incredibly, however, the stereotype that too many people still carry unexamined is the untrue myth that homosexuals are *the* pedophiles.[26] An editorial in Portland's *Oregonian* newspaper recognized that this misinformation was being used as a scare tactic to attempt to get people to vote for the 1992 Ballot Measure 9, which would have made homosexuality, hiring of homosexuals, providing books or studies or media that were at all positive of homosexuality, and more, illegal in the state of Oregon. The editorial, entitled "No shield from predators: Parents shouldn't assume that Measure 9 would rid schools of potential sexual abusers," read in part:

> The Oregon Citizens Alliance [which sponsored Ballot Measure 9] links homosexuality with pedophiles in Ballot Measure 9, which condemns both, but parents and others who want to protect children against sexual abuse should not follow them in that flawed leap of logic.
> If they do, their children will be on guard against an enemy that rarely exists and be less able to spot the ones that do.

Most children who are sexually abused are abused by a parent or a relative. Very few cases involve strangers, and very few pedophiles are also homosexuals, says A. Nicholas Groth, a Florida psychologist.

Groth is an expert on sexual abuse and its prevention, a consultant to child sexual-abuse intervention programs, and author of a book on the sexual assault of children and adolescents.

He was in Portland . . . to participate in an international conference on male survivors of sexual abuse. Most of the 200 or so participants were therapists and counselors who deal with boys and men who have been sexually abused.

'There is no research link between homosexuality and pedophilia,' Gross told the Oregonian's editorial board, adding that in his more than 25 years of work he has encountered no case in which a gay person abandoned a same-sex partner in order to abuse a child.

It's not uncommon for pedophiles to choose victims of either sex, opportunistically selecting the child who seems least likely to report the abuse. Men who abuse young boys are not homosexuals, Groth said, they are pedophiles.

The danger of parents linking the two is that they may be so watchful for signs of sexual abuse by a homosexual counselor or teacher that they miss the more likely candidates—their own relatives, family, friends or neighbors.

If children are led to believe that homosexuals or some other scary people 'out there' are the ones they should fear, they won't be prepared to deal with attempted abuse from someone who does not fit the stereotype. . . .

In short, Measure 9 offers children no protection. Instead, it leaves them ill-prepared to deal with the real sexual predators they may encounter. *(Oregonian,* September 18, 1992)

All children must be protected from all pedophiles. But society's misunderstandings about child sexual abuse are compounding efforts not only to protect children, but also to detect, arrest, and treat abusers.

Though the act of sexual violation—sexual abuse—is increasingly understood as an act of violence against the child (with sex the weapon) and not, in fact, an act of sex for sexuality's sake, that distinction is difficult to maintain.

When considering men abusing girls, using sexual acts as a weapon, far too often public opinion and court cases can still hinge on whether the girl child "asked for" the man's sexual violation in some way, and whether perhaps the man was just being sexually responsive to the female's "seductive behavior." The distinction between violence using sex *versus* a man's sexually responsive behavior gets clouded, and it's too often a struggle to clarify that the child in no way asked for or could ever "deserve" such violation from the larger, more powerful adult. The fact that violence was the crux of what occurred too often gets lost behind the focus on the sexual acts involved.

In attempted murder cases, do the courts focus on, "In what way did you ask to be assaulted? What did you do so the perpetrator chose to attack you with a rifle? Why didn't he use a knife? Or poison?" Focusing on the weapon of the crime instead of the violence itself—the means of the crime instead of the fact that there was an assault—seems incongruous in that setting. But unfortunately for victims of child sexual assault, the opposite is too often true.

So perhaps it should be no surprise that when men abuse boys with sexual acts as the weapon, the vital distinction between violence using sex and sexually responsive behavior is even harder to keep clear. Since consensual same-gender sexual behavior is so taboo, and homophobia is so rampant, any same-gender sexual behavior is generally not thought through objectively in the best of times. So in a crisis such as child abuse, it's almost certain to receive knee-jerk stereotypic reactions that serve unconscionably to attack the child in yet another unbearable way.

If a boy is sexually abused by an adult male, society's handy but misinformed stereotype is that the boy, too, may have in some way asked for it, just as girls are stereotypically suspected of having provoked their abuse.

Even in households where a father abuses both girl and boy children, the focus on the man as a clearly violent person who attacks weaker dependents with sexual weapons seems not to be grasped clearly enough.

Instead, the sexual framework of the violation takes on primary focus. Girls suffer the attack, the terror, and the reprimands of being perhaps too feminine. Boys suffer the attack and the terror too, but also meet head-on an assault on their very "maleness," and are accused either directly or indirectly of being not-male or not male enough. They meet head-on society's fear and hatred of homosexual people and find themselves included in that ostracized group solely for the fact that they have suffered sexual assault from another male.

The doubly compounded issue is almost more than the child can bear. The boy has suffered violence. But with sex being its weapon, and society's focus more on the sex than on the violence, the boy, too, is left to focus on the sexual act and what it means to who he is or will be in the future.

Of course opposite-gender sexual abuse by mothers, female baby sitters and others is also an affront to a boy's "maleness," as opposite-gender abuse of girls, by men, is an affront to their "femaleness," with those intrusions on their developing sexuality being tremendously difficult to confront and resolve, at best, should they decide finally to speak of it.

But for both boy and girl children who endured same-gender abuse, the extra layer of homophobia is also poised to crash down upon them if and when they finally decide to speak out.

If society were more tolerant of the full range of consensual sexual behaviors people do experience in a lifetime and weren't so harsh on consensual same-gender experiences, children would not have to undergo this additional severe layer of pain upon suddenly finding themselves tied to a suspect group status.

To escape tags such as "fag" or "queer," boys, in particular, who are old enough to recognize the dangers of being aligned in any way with same-gender sex can find it somehow safer to remain silent, and decide to pass in a different way—as not suffering from such sexual violence—rather than to speak up and seek help.

As long as society allows and maintains its blanket mistreatment of homosexual people in society, there's no safe haven for boys to flee to in order to express and recover from their experiences of same-gender sexual abuse.

It's reasonable to suspect that many boys survive their abuse in part by blocking it out of their conscious memories until late adulthood, as many women now find they have done. The difference between the adult women and men who do remember their abuse later on is that the women, now, are often encouraged to go to counseling professionals and the courts to seek healing and sometimes even legal recourse. Men, on the other hand, often cannot imagine speaking to another person about the experiences they're remembering, fearing that they'll inadvertently take on society's rejection of homosexuals and the negative stigma gay men suffer, if they do dare speak up. So, in the face of painful memories that need healing release, they instead pass silently by, allowing other aspects of their life to suffer rather than seek help to heal the core pain they've uncovered.

Of course, not all men who are vocally anti-gay had to have been sexually abused as children. Other factors such as verbal abuse, strong anti-gay peer pressure, or strongly negative religious training can cause prejudiced behavior, too.

But how many men who do behave so voraciously anti-gay are doing so because of either conscious or unconscious experiences of abuse they dare not tell to anyone? For how many is their absolute condemnation of homosexual persons a desperate attempt to insure that everyone around soundly understands that they're in *no way* affiliated with that despised group?

Once again, prejudice reduction theory can illuminate their struggle (NCBI). An example would be a man who suffered (remembered or unremembered) ridicule and accusations of being gay after he was sexually abused by his father. Now, he verbally attacks anyone who appears gay. Unfortunately, each attack on others brings up the unresolved wounds about the childhood attack on himself. The resulting rush of emotions is interpreted as hatred of those others, when, in fact, his emotional feelings are so strong in part because they rub an open wound within. As he continues hurting others in the way he himself was hurt, he's trapped in a cycle that will continue until (if and when) he faces his original hurt and attains a level of healing and peace within himself.

The healing can only begin when the adult can *know* that as a boy he in no way deserved to be sexually violated. Whether as an adult he turned out to be heterosexual or homosexual, he shouldn't have feared or experienced attacks on his maleness just at the time he was being most violated. He didn't deserve the violence; he didn't deserve to be additionally attacked due to society's misunderstanding and irrational fear about same-gender consensual sex. He didn't deserve to be treated so badly. And once he can truly believe that, he can also begin to believe that no one else should be treated badly on either count either. His violent treatment of homosexuals can end when he no longer feels his very survival is dependent upon keeping them and their persecution as far away from himself as possible.

The prejudice reduction theory, come full circle, leads to one of the golden rules that is otherwise lost in acts of prejudice. This Golden Rule is to 'do unto others as you would have them do unto you.' But as long as people are hurting others because of what they themselves suffered, they are in fact doing unto others *what has been done unto them.* In the process, they hurt themselves anew with every attack aimed at the other's behavior, since they haven't recovered from their own painful connection with similar circumstances.

Only when the basis of such pain is addressed and healed can the person who did, in fact, suffer hurt choose not to cultivate it onward into posterity. Only with the recognition that personal pain only ends when it is *not* perpetuated can people then choose to do unto others what they would have others do unto them.

As long as male *children* continue to view staying in a sexually abusive relationship as being less damaging than confronting society's pervasive mistreatment of anyone perceived as homosexual, they'll continue to pay the price of not being able to seek safety. They allow their violent mistreatment to pass unaddressed and, thus, suffer needlessly. Society suffers not only for them, but must suffer later as well since some of these same unsupported male children may, in turn, become adults who might abuse girl and/or boy children. Since they themselves couldn't seek help as children, they remain caught up in continuing a cycle of violence that must be stopped, for everyone's sake.

As long as men who, *in later adulthood*, do remember their abuse but refuse to seek help and healing for fear of facing condemnation or retribution for being in some way connected with behaviors that would lead some to accuse them of being homosexual, they also pay the price of letting their pain pass silently. They, too, will continue to suffer needlessly, and in turn might hate and mistreat actual homosexual people, thus perpetuating the very societal non-acceptance that put them into their painful bind in the first place.

And, lastly, adult men who are *in present time* sexually abusing male children will have almost no inclination to seek help in stopping their violent behavior since they know they'd be opening themselves up not just to the issues of child abuse, but also to charges of homosexuality and all the legal and social attacks such accusations bring. If, in fact, their adult consensual sex is with women, and they believe themselves to be heterosexual, they can feel they have far too much to lose to have the accusation of being homosexual thrown at them. So they also pass, silent even if they might wish they could seek help to stop their abusive behavior, for fear the repercussions of homosexual accusations would be more unendurable than those of child assault.

The cycle of sexual violence against all children must be broken. Its component of homophobia must be recognized as an aggravating element that drives many people to silence, not healing, in the face of their pain. The ramifications of homophobia must be alleviated if the cycle is truly to be broken. Men must be free to speak of the abuse they suffered so as to be able to seek counsel, and so they will be less apt as adults to abuse girl and/or boy children.

So once again, it's vitally necessary for society to move beyond its silences about homosexuality so that gay, lesbian, and bi people are free to speak up safely, be themselves, and resoundingly end the untrue stereotypes that currently govern too many people's negative views of them. Until it's clear that there are good people and bad people of *every* sexual orientation, stereotypical biases will continue to trap children and adults alike in far too many ongoing violent situations.

Fear of homosexuals must pass away so that the real issues at hand can be addressed, so that children can be protected, and so that children and adults alike can find safe harbors where they can seek and find healing.

Perpetuating Fear

Where there is fear we lose the way of our spirit.
~ *Gandhi*

Perhaps the most pervasive price society pays for its insistence that everyone pass as always/only heterosexual, and as always/only in one certain gender, is the perpetuation of a pervasive undercurrent of unnecessary fear.

Fear *of* one another

Much discussion has already taken place about the burden of fear sexual minority people carry constantly: fear for their safety, fear that heterosexuals will do them harm.

This fear often is warranted, since few laws are in place to protect them from attack or losses when accused of being sexually outside "the norm." By 2002, only twelve states and the District of Columbia protected people from employment discrimination on the basis of sexual orientation. Fewer still offer protection on the basis of gender-identity or behavior. And until 2003 thirteen states still criminalized same-gender consensual sex even in the privacy of one's own home.

Thus in most of the United States, people can be and are perfectly legally not hired, fired, denied housing, denied public accommodation, and denied benefits simply because they are or are presumed to be non-heterosexual. Since transgender people are almost always grouped with homosexuals because they, too, are deemed sexually "different" (regardless of their actual sexual orientation), they, too, are denied the same legal protections withheld from homosexuals due to the anti-gay prejudices of the day.

Thus many people live in fear of exposure, silent about their lives, hoping to avoid harm. However, as long as these millions of law-abiding contributing members of society do choose to pass for their safety, the bulk of the balance of society is left to carry, unchallenged, its own fear of the frightening stereotypes "those [undesirable] homosexuals" bring to mind.

The negative, frightening stereotype painted of bisexual, lesbian, and gay people as unstable, child-molesting, and undependable people on the periphery of the law is a scary one. With only negative stereotypes in hand, uninformed persons are left to carry a constant fear that "those people" must be avoided at all costs and must preferably be kept separate from the rest of society for society's sake.

Any inklings that a person might be bi or gay or lesbian, or fears that such people might be involved in a work or community project, are enough to send some people heading for shelter with genuine terror in their hearts. Any oddities about someone they don't know can cause walls of distrust to go up as a safety mechanism in the face of possibly being around such a stereotypically-defined danger.

When my mother testified for an equal rights ordinance for lesbian and gay citizens of Anchorage, Alaska, in October of 1989, she articulated the needless quandary well:

> We're locked in a stereotype view of gay persons. It's not homosexuality itself that's wrong, but our attitude toward it. We lump all gay persons in the same boat and then paint the picture using the lowest common denominator. Wouldn't we 'straight' people be up in arms if anyone lumped all of us together and took as the 'norm' the lowest possible denominator? (Boesser, Mildred. Testimony at Anchorage Assembly. 1989)

It's bad enough to know that there are, in fact, dangerous people out in society who do harm to others. But to harbor such fear of an entire group of people has proved historically, over and over again, to be unrealistic and unnecessary. Within each "group" of people is the full range of good to bad. Unfortunately, with the majority of lesbian, bi, and gay people passing as heterosexual, the blatant untruths of the homosexual stereotype aren't being fully challenged and unseated.

According to the 1990 Kinsey report,

> In one national poll, only one-quarter of the adults responding said that they had a homosexual friend or acquaintance. Of course they could only respond about those they knew about! This means that three-quarters of American adults probably base their opinions about homosexuals on stereotypes. (Reinisch with Beasley, 1990, p. 148)

Since sexuality is generally an invisible quality about a person, these unchallenged, scary stereotypes haunt the majority of people in a number of ways:

1) If a person who *is* gay or lesbian or bi is "out" enough for people to accurately spot that orientation, people afraid of the stereotypes are automatically distrustful if not fearful of the person—regardless of how trustworthy the person actually is.

2) If it appears that a person *might* be bi or lesbian or gay, but in fact isn't, the people afraid of the stereotype suffer in exactly the same way. Since there's no way of confirming their suspicions other than direct questioning, and since it's generally unthinkable to get close enough to a suspectedly dangerous person to ask such a question, the fearful person is left with only their unspoken suspicions and the resulting discomfort, distrust, or even terror.

3) Even when a person appears to be *hetero*sexual, enough of the general public is aware that passing takes place to cause some people to remain at a level of almost constant distrust, as in examples where a parent might automatically fear for their child just in case their child's teacher might be gay.

   In reality, though, with one in four girls being sexually abused by adult men they know in their life, heterosexual status is absolutely no guarantee that any given teacher is "safe." In other words, to attempt truly to protect children, parents should instead focus on the teacher's character, not on possible sexual orientation. Homosexuals are not *the* child abusers; rather, *pedophiles*—of any sexual orientation—are the child abusers. Fear on the basis of sexual orientation is a needless, unrelated layer of fear that could be eliminated.

4) The heterosexual majority itself lives in fear they might not be perceived as *heterosexual enough* by their colleagues, so they also live with a constant threshold of fear they might not measure up enough to be a "real man" or a "real woman." Generally unvoiced is the underlying, almost subconscious, fear that they might suffer from society's oppressive treatment of homosexuals if they don't find and maintain ways to measure up.

5) Fear of getting "too close" to a person of the same gender is a final manifestation of fear far too many people live with. Women in our culture are allowed to be more intimate with other women than men are with men. For men in particular, intimate nonsexual friendships outside very limited settings (such as sports, war, and religious brotherhoods) are practically taboo.

But both genders know that to go beyond the boundaries of "acceptable" closeness, even when no sexual activity is in the picture, puts them in danger of negative societal reactions. To insure they don't cross the line, friendships are limited, and any attempts by either party to be a closer friend are automatically viewed with suspicion or fear by the friend and/or by onlookers to the friendship.

Recently I was at a gathering where two heterosexual young women were marveling to several friends about how deep their friendship with one another was becoming. One said, "I just love everything about her; it's almost scary." The other stated, "I've never been this close to a girl friend before. It's frightening." Clearly neither was afraid of the other. They obviously adored one another and loved the time they spent together. Instead, their fright had a deeper, almost subconscious root: they could sense their feelings went deeper than cultural norms expected. Their fear was actually for their own safety if they allowed this feeling of taboo intimacy to continue.

At a union meeting, for another example, I overheard a conversation down the row of chairs from me. One man had come early and already had a seat. Another man from his department came in and they greeted each other warmly. But as the one entering took his seat by his friend, he left one chair between them, saying, "I'll sit here so no one will think we're at all funny." ("Funny" being another euphemism for gay.) Avoiding trouble; fear in action. The end result: distance between the men—figuratively, symbolically, and, in the end, literally. How much time would they ever choose to spend together in genuine friendship if they couldn't even safely sit next to one another at a public meeting?

Fear is the limiting factor in all five scenarios. Initially, heterosexual people believe they fear homosexuals. But oft-unknown to themselves, they fear other heterosexuals as well, and fear even their own behavior—afraid that it might not pass muster as being above reproach.

These unrecognized threads of fear are everywhere. And as long as the scary, negative, *untrue* stereotypes of homosexuals are allowed to go unchallenged and unremedied, this pervasive fear will prevail. If lesbian, gay, and bisexual people felt free to come out safely and expose the falsity of the stereotypes, everyone could relax. And everyone would benefit.

Fear *for* one another

Sexual minority people fear heterosexual people. Heterosexual people fear sexual minority people, one another, and even themselves. And there is one additional layer of fear that must be mentioned. That is the fear both sides have not *of*, but *for* the other.

When both my parents volunteered to testify in 1989 in support of a gay/lesbian equal rights ordinance in Anchorage, Alaska, my initial reaction was tremendous gratitude. But as I began to work on my three-minute testimony, I realized that part of me questioned their participation.

They were three years from retirement, pastoring a small church in a nearby town. While their national church, the Episcopal church, had taken a positive stand in support of lesbian and gay persons being full and equal members of God's creation and worthy of protection by secular laws, not everyone in their specific congregation felt that way.

My mother had jokingly remarked, "Well, if they don't like it [their testifying], we can always retire three years early!" A courageous statement—especially in the face of its possible truth and possible dire consequences (a pastor they knew from another denomination had been fired after coming out in support of lesbian and gay persons). What if they were to lose their parish, forced to retire early at a reduced income for the rest of their lives (having not made it to age sixty-five for full benefits)? What if such a controversy came up that they had to end their forty-plus year career on a hurtful, painful note, instead of with the love and respect of those they'd served for so long?

If any issue could do them in, it was this. They knew it and I knew it, though we only touched on it in conversation, hoping deep down it was an unreasonable fear.

But when I presented my testimony, my parents were on my mind just as much as the anti-discrimination ordinance at hand. I knew it was important for the politicians and members of the public present to hear what I chose to speak about:

> Courage is the flip side of fear; fear is the *bottom line* in discrimination. You ask for proof of discrimination? Fear is the major proof you will find.
>
> I stand before you tonight an incredibly fortunate person. I'm fortunate because I have both my parents here with me tonight. They fear greatly for my safety.
>
> But you know, I have as much fear *for them*, here, at this moment. They're my parents, and I want them safe. I don't want them hurt in any way because of this stand they're taking. But they know, I know, the discrimination exists. We fear it, yet tonight we face it together. (Boesser, Sara. Testimony at Anchorage Assembly. 1989.)

The Anchorage ordinance did not pass—it was shelved indefinitely for "more study." Gratefully, my parents didn't suffer my worst fears for their courage in coming out in support of it. Nor did I suffer any losses for being an openly lesbian spokesperson for its passage. But the overall fear has lessened only gradually. The three of us have testified a number of times since then for fair and equal treatment of all citizens, including gay, lesbian, bi, intersexual, and trans people, and a degree of fear is always palpable.

While it seemed appropriate to me to wish to protect my parents, it wasn't until about a year later that I came to realize an aspect of passing I'd been oblivious to. At an allies-building workshop ("allies" being heterosexual persons who support fair and equal treatment of homosexual, bisexual, transgender, and intersexual people), I was asked, "What prevents you from organizing your allies to come to your assistance" [i.e., what prevents me from asking supportive heterosexuals to speak up in support of lesbian/bi/gay/trans/inter rights]? Without forethought, I stated succinctly, "I don't want my allies to be hurt."

In other words, while I wanted—and desperately needed—their help in counterbalancing all the negative press and negative stereotypes, I was unwilling to subject them to the possible attacks I recognized they might well suffer for coming to our defense. I felt many of them were blind to what could befall them, and I wished to protect them from the attacks they were opening themselves up to if they did place themselves in allegiance with such an unmistakably despised group.

My protection in part was out of concern for their safety. But upon further reflection, I realized another issue was at stake: if they, in fact, did get hurt as a result of contradicting the myths and stereotypes about homosexuals, they might decide it wasn't worth the trouble—that *we* weren't worth the trouble—and they might at best abandon us as allies. At worst, perhaps they'd even jump ship entirely and also begin to attack us in order to avoid ever being hurt personally over the issue again.

In other words, I was so busy protecting heterosexuals I was unable to be an effective leader of those who truly did want to work to end the vicious cycle. My lack of trust and my fear of potential loss of "protected" allies were, in the end, short-circuiting any advancements we all might make together.

Where had this sense of almost mandatory responsibility to protect heterosexuals come from? If it came from some unverbalized belief that they'd be grateful for how I'd kept them from harm, it turned out nothing could be further from the truth. Instead, once I began to communicate more in depth with my allies, I realized my silence about our hurts and dangers had been so effective that my allies actually had no idea the extent of the discrimination we experience. They therefore had no basis on which to comprehend the danger I sensed for them. I had instead taken away not only their recognition of the gravity of the situation, but more importantly had robbed them of their own choice in how to meet it. My silence, compounded by my protection, had immobilized my allies.

In 1990, the city council in Juneau, Alaska, reviewed an ordinance that would extend non-discrimination protections to city workers on a number of bases, including that of sexual orientation. Going into the ordinance process in my home town, once again as a visibly open lesbian spokesperson, I had no idea who would rise to speak with and for us. I didn't dare set my hopes too high, and at the time was unaware of my technique of protecting my heterosexual friends and allies. But an astounding thing happened that changed forever my view of being isolated from assistance.

Several supporters of the ordinance devised a petition that a few people would carry by hand to gather signatures, and the signatures were to be printed in a large display ad in our local newspaper. It was a daring idea—to have people's names in print in support of fair and equal treatment for all, not just on the basis of age, sex, race, disability, marital and parental status, etc.—but also sexual orientation.

Those last two words were, of course, the ones I feared no one would or could ally themselves with in public. And, left only to my own devices, I wouldn't have proposed such a goal.

But I learned an important lesson. Over and over again, hetero-sexual friends—and even acquaintances and co-workers—repeatedly said, "I'm so glad there's something I can do," and "thank you for asking me to sign this." In less than two weeks, a handful of people had gathered almost six hundred signatures. A press deadline was all that stopped the flow. It was a memorable moment, and I learned powerfully that sexual minority people are not alone in this issue, that others can and will take their own risks when given a choice. And they'll thank me for it. It changed my life.

This is not to say that none of the signers suffered harm. One (heterosexual) woman's sibling's family refused to speak to her for years after the ordinance process. Another worked with one of the leaders of the opposition, and found working relations very difficult afterwards. She has since sought and secured another job. I don't know everyone on the signature list; and I cannot know all their follow-up stories. I hope they're all well and safe; but I'm now willing to allow that they can take their own risks and survive their own results. They, like me, can take action and can survive.

The fear *for* one another works the other way, too. People who are friends and allies of bi, lesbian, intersexual, transgender, and gay people do fear for our safety. And those who care the most tend to look to their sexual minority friends or relatives for clues as to how best to support us.

When they see us passing, not speaking our reality, they frequently follow our lead. If in conversations where an anti-gay joke comes up and their lesbian friend makes no comment to challenge it, the ally lets it pass also. If a gay friend shows no outrage when the local newspaper uses negative stereotypes about homosexuals in a news story, then his friends remains silent as well. They're aware their homosexual friend is struggling to pass for safety, and because they care, the heterosexual allies also strive to in no way rock the boat and create danger unintentionally. As a result, following the lesbian or gay person's lead, the heterosexual person may intentionally pass, too, passing as someone who does not know or care about a person who is b/g/l/i/t.

In other cases, a b/g/l/t/i person who does speak honestly to a heterosexual confidant sometimes intentionally asks that heterosexual friend not to speak directly or even indirectly of the conversations. While heterosexual friends can be grateful for being trusted enough to hear the other's truth, they can be unprepared for then finding themselves unexpectedly also caught in the web of passing's silence, finding out only after the fact that their silence is also expected to extend into and throughout the rest of their lives.

Janis's story is not unusual. Married, in her late thirties, and mother of a young son, she spoke at length with me about some of her earlier memories, thinking back to when she first realized she knew someone who was lesbian or gay. First she remembered a junior high girl friend who entrusted her realizations about herself to Janis. Then she remembered her mother telling her of a member of her church who'd realized he was gay after many years of marriage. Then she remembered a date in high school with an older young man who had attended seminary for some years before dropping out, who told her there had been a number of young seminarians who discovered they were gay, and how painful that was for them. Suddenly Janis stopped speaking, then hesitantly began again, clearly startled by what she was recalling:

> My boyfriend talked about it a lot, about those young men finding out they were gay and that it was a pretty painful situation. Oh, and as a matter of fact, my boyfriend—my boyfriend himself told me he had had a lover in seminary, and it was one of the most painful memories he had because he didn't know what to do about it. He told me never to tell anybody—and I've never mentioned it at all—till now! Wow! It's amazing how these memories become lost. I never said anything, not once. Because he was somebody I loved, and he described it with such pain, I remember believing that there was *love* there. And I could personally understand from my own experience the spiritual struggle of being something yet not being able to express it. That was very powerful to me, that this man loved another man. But like I say, I never spoke about it, and it really bothered me, something so important under this ban of silence.

Friends, then, also pass—by being silent—for fear that to speak at all might be to say too much and endanger someone they care about. By following the silent lead of friends who pass or by respecting their stated request that silence be maintained, allies find their hands tied, too. And they have no role models of how to work to end the oppressions that make the passing seem necessary in the first place.

It's a circular, never-ending loop that can only be broken as new models become available. The new model, of course, is to not pass. When transgender, intersexual, gay, bi, and lesbian people cease to pass and are open about who they fully are, that openness will free their friends and allies to be open also. If a person has nothing to hide, there's nothing to protect, and fully truthful and uncensored discussion can finally occur.

Additionally, as more heterosexual people learn to not pass as only/always heterosexual and come out *for themselves*, they'll realize that they can speak up without endangering those they care about. As they state ways in which it will be better *for themselves*—let alone everyone else—if this society-wide mistreatment ends, they'll realize they can make a difference without ever mentioning the personal confidences they carry inside.

This move beyond passing is in process daily. Its emergence takes many forms; and it's a vital movement if we are to accept the fact that not only is passing not best for everyone, but rather *not passing* is best for us all.

> We pass:
> we lie
> at first to hide
> from others;
> then we cross the lie'n find
> we're hiding
> from ourselves.
>
> ~ *Sara Boesser, 1994*

Reflections—

15. "As long as society allows and maintains its blanket mistreatment of homosexual people in society, there's no safe haven for boys to flee to in order to express and recover from their experiences of same-gender sexual abuse. . . . They allow their violent mistreatment to pass unaddressed and, thus, suffer needlessly. Society suffers not only for them, but must suffer later as well since some of these same unsupported male children may, in turn, become adults who might abuse girl and/or boy children. Since they themselves couldn't seek help as children, they remain caught up in continuing a cycle of violence that must be stopped, for everyone's sake."

    a. How would you react if you heard a girl child had been sexually abused? A boy child?

    b. Do you know a man or woman who was sexually abused as a child? When did they finally tell someone? How were they treated by people they told? By other people who found out?

    c. How do you think the media treats the issue of child sexual abuse of girls? Of boys?

16. "This Golden Rule is to do unto others as you would have them do unto you. But as long as people are hurting others because of what they themselves suffered, they are in fact doing unto others *what has been done unto them*. In the process, they hurt themselves anew with every attack aimed at the other's behavior, since they haven't recovered from their own painful connection with similar circumstances."

    a. Generally, how do you treat others when you're angry with them?

    b. Was there a family member or other significant person in your life who, when they were angry, treated you in a particularly hurtful way when you were a child?

    c.   How did that treatment feel when you were a child?

    d.   Is there anything you'd like to be able to say to that person today about how it felt?

    e.   Do you ever find yourself treating others that way when you're angry?

    f.   How do you wish you'd been treated by that person when they were angry with you when you were a child?

17. "It's bad enough to know that there are, in fact, dangerous people out in society who would do harm to others. But to harbor such fear of an entire group of people has proved, historically, over and over again, to be unrealistic and unnecessary."

    a.   What groups are you a member of? (A few examples: gender, race, ethnicity, parental status, age, physical build status, physical abilities status, employment status, military status, economic status, religion, first language, hairstyle, handedness, political party, personality type, hobbies, interests.) List as many for yourself as possible.

    b.   Are you aware of anyone or any groups of people that might find any of the groups you belong to undesirable, threatening, or dangerous?

    c.   In history, or today, have any of the groups with whom you have membership been attacked or maligned by any other group? In America? Elsewhere in the world?

    d.   What reasons were/are given for blanket disregard or attack of groups you belong to?

    e.   How does it feel that others may fear or even hate parts of yourself (i.e., group affiliations you have)?

    f.   How many of your group membership statuses are a matter of choice (examples: marital status, religious affiliation)? How many are not a choice? What difference, if any, do you think this distinction makes to those who attack the group?

g. Picture a person, known or imaginary, who might hate a group to which you belong. What might that person say to you about the reason(s) they fear or hate you? What would you like to say to that person?

18. "These unrecognized threads of fear are everywhere. And as long as the scary, negative, *untrue* stereotypes of homosexuals are allowed to go unchallenged and unremedied, this pervasive fear will prevail. If lesbian, gay, and bisexual people were free safely to come out and expose the falsity of the stereotypes, everyone could relax. And everyone would benefit."

a. Think back to the groups you belong to that you listed earlier. What are the negative, untrue stereotypes for those groups?

b. Do you fit the negative stereotype traits attributed to all your groups?

19. "as the one entering took his seat by his friend, he left one chair between them, saying, 'I'll sit here so no one will think we're at all funny.' 'Funny': another euphemism for gay. Avoiding trouble; fear in action. The end result: distance between the men: figuratively, symbolically, and, in the end, literally. How much time would they ever choose to spend together in genuine friendship if they couldn't even safely sit next to one another in a public meeting?"

19-1: *For heterosexuals:*

a. If you have (or had) a close same-gender friend, what activities are you comfortable doing together with *only* the two of you (no double dates, no three- or more groups)? Why?

b. When the two of you are together with other people, are there any ways in which you consciously or unconsciously protect your friendship from the outside perception of possible homo-sexuality, as the two men above did? How does that feel?

19-2: *For lesbians, gays, and bi's*:

a.   If you have (or had) a close opposite-gender friend, what activities are you comfortable doing together with *only* the two of you (no double dates, no three- or more- groups)? Why?

b.   When the two of you (opposite-gender friends) are together with other people, are there any ways in which you consciously or unconsciously protect your friendship from the outside perception of presumed heterosexuality, so that gay and lesbian friends won't assume it's a date? How does this feel?

    Or, conversely, do you ever encourage people who are heterosexual to presume the friendship *is* of intimate het-erosexual relationship status? How does that feel?

20. "I was so busy protecting heterosexuals, I was unable to be an effective leader of those who truly did want to work to end the vicious cycle. My lack of trust and my fear of potential loss of 'protected' allies were, in the end, short-circuiting any advance-ments we all might make together."

20-1: *For bi's, lesbian, trans, inters, and gays*:

a.   Do you have close heterosexual friends (other than family)? If not, why do you think you don't?

b.   If you are close to heterosexual friends or family and are out to them, have you told them how personally difficult it is to live in a homophobic/gender-restricted society? Have you been specific? Have you told them bad things that have happened to you or to sexual minority people you know? If you haven't told them, why not?

c.   Have you shared any of your difficult realities with supportive co-workers? If not, why not?

d. Have you ever told friends, family, or allies of your difficulties, followed by pledging them to silence? Have they honored that request?

e. Have you ever spoken out against anti-gay/trans/inter statements or actions? Have you ever written a letter to the editor in support of sexual minority issues? Have you ever testified for a sexual minority cause? Has your family member or friend or co-worker ever done any of these things?

f. Would you feel comfortable going to your heterosexual friend, family member, or coworker for help if you were attacked or threatened in any way because of your sexual orientation? Because of your gender identity or behavior? Your intersexual status? If not, why not?

20-2: *For heterosexuals:*

a. Do you know if you have close homosexual, bisexual, transgender, or intersexual friends or family? If you think you don't, can you imagine why you might not be told if, in fact, some of your friends or family actually are?

b. If you do know a friend, family member, or co-worker is l/b/i/t/g, is that person out to you? If not, why do you imagine this to be so?

c. If that person *is* out to you, have you ever asked questions or encouraged conversation about their life, or asked about the discrimination they or their friends might face?

d. If a friend did come out to you about their sexual minority status, but asked you to share nothing about the disclosure, has that affected your ability to address the lesbian/gay/trans/bi/ intersexual issue? How might you honor that pledge and still speak from your own perspective without in any way endangering your friend?

e.   Have you ever made positive comments about sexual orientation or gender identity rights in the presence of others where that friend could hear you?

f.   Have you ever spoken out against anti-gay/trans/inter statements or actions? Have you ever written a letter to the editor in support of sexual minority issues? Have you ever testified for a sexual minority cause? Has your sexual minority friend or co-worker ever done any of these things?

g.   Would you want your non-heterosexual, transgender, or intersexual friend or family member to call you for help if s/he were attacked in some way because of her/his status?

Conclusion:

Silent No More

9. The Personal

Passing is a high price for individuals and for society to pay. Whether it's done for safety, for job security, or to avoid violence or discrimination—even when it's successful—both the individual and society pay a price, from loss of personal integrity to the nation's failure to live up to its own standards of fair and equal treatment of all its citizens.

As long as people pass, the societal stereotypes condemning everything except only-heterosexual orientation/behavior will remain unchallenged, and mistreatment of people who are or who are suspected of being lesbian, gay, intersexual, transgender, or bisexual will be perpetuated.

Failure to confront and end the pressures that enforce passing in turn affects every single other member of society as well, from limitations of acceptable gender role options both personally and professionally, to limitations on ending sexual abuse and serving victims of it, to perpetuation of unnecessary fear.

Every single member of society would in fact benefit from an end to the need for passing. If anti-g/l/b/t/i prejudice were no longer condoned, every single member of society would be spared the degree of oppression they personally endure whether they recognize it or not.

The fear involved that causes passing is tremendous.

As I wrote in my October 4, 1988, National Coming Out Day[27] editorial for the *Juneau Empire*, "Our country has a long and continuing history of facing and re-evaluating its prejudices and forms of discrimination. Anyone who chooses to question such prejudices, who is out of step with the prevailing accepted norms, finds it no easy task."

Easy to break the silence? No. But silence can become unbearable when the price in loss of integrity finally becomes too great.

Over time, gay, intersexual, bisexual, transgender, and lesbian people are finding the courage to "come out"—no longer to pass—with greater and greater frequency. Of course they must choose carefully how and with whom to take that risk.

But heterosexual people, too, are now realizing that they also must come out and must themselves refuse to pass as well. They too must refuse to let the untrue stereotypes and hateful myths prevail, if passing and its almost endless repercussions are to fade from the norm in our society. To urge them on, in the same editorial I wrote:

> How do heterosexuals come out?
>
> What do you do to show your support? You could say to someone you know well, someone you trust, 'I know and care about someone who is a lesbian.' Or, 'I respect someone who is gay.' Or, 'I wanted to tell you that I am related to someone who is bisexual. I love that person very much.'
>
> *Don't use their names*—it's not necessary. In fact, it's best not to name them because the person you're speaking of would prefer to tell people about themselves when they're ready to do so. You are coming out *for yourself.* You've personalized it enough by saying, 'I know someone who is . . . and I care about them.'
>
> By saying just that much, you have made a significant difference for the friend or relative you care about. You have added to the growing base of understanding and support that is invaluable to them as they continue to come out for themselves. (Boesser, Sara. *Juneau Empire*, 1988)

And each person who speaks up is also making a significant additional difference for every heterosexual member of society as well. The growing base of support for openly g/l/b/t/i people is the same base of support that will also make society safer for heterosexual people who dare to be true to themselves and think or act in some way outside society's current restrictive gender role norms.

Coming out is like Rosa Parks
going to the front of the bus:
until she did that, nothing changed.
~ Carol Zimmerman, 1993

10. The Political

In addition to taking opportunities to speak out and not pass—to come out whenever it's safe to do so personally either as a heterosexual supporter or as a bisexual, gay, transgender, intersexual, or lesbian individual—it's vital that everyone support the expansion of equal rights laws to prohibit discrimination based on sexual orientation and gender identity/behavior. Such laws don't come easy. My mother's 1989 testimony to the Anchorage Human Rights Commission stated the painful discordance of the status quo succinctly:

> I see the expansion of legal rights for lesbians and gay men as a step forward and a move away from our present hypocrisy, which allows gay persons equal rights to a job and a place to live so long as they do not admit their sexual orientation. In other words, lie about yourself, about the way God made you, and you'll be treated fairly, but tell the truth about yourself and your life will be an endless nightmare. (Boesser, Mildred. Testimony to Anchorage Assembly. 1989.)

According to English philosopher John Stewart Mill, "Every great movement must experience three stages: ridicule, discussion, adoption." The struggle for extending existing human rights protections to sexual minority citizens is as emotionally charged and difficult as any civil rights issue to date. Today it's increasingly in the news media, and more and more people are finding themselves consciously thinking about the issues. If discussion is the second stage in every great social movement, then our nation finds itself in the second stage today.

But valuable discussion cannot occur if some of the parties involved are silent. Opponents to equal rights for all regardless of sexual minority status often vehemently say, "You can do whatever you like in private—just don't talk about it! And don't ask us to put the words 'sexual orientation' or 'gender expression and identity' in our nondiscrimination laws, media, or textbooks."

This attitude is not unlike early days of the African-American civil rights movement, where people grudgingly said, "Blacks can have rights, just so they don't 'get uppity.'" In other words, as African-Americans were begrudgingly given their rights under law, the tacit insistence was that they must nonetheless keep their place—their place of *subservience*.

Today sexual minority citizens find themselves in the same catch-22: we're told we'll be left alone to live our lives relatively safely if we keep our place, and our place is *silence*.

Subservience, silence—neither should be the price of safety. And neither is the essence of freedom. The imposition of either means that persons suffering the oppression have fewer actual rights than other citizens.

So the opponents who urge supporters of equal rights for sexual orientation and gender identity to maintain silence are attempting to set up ground rules under which no true discussion can possibly take place. Such ground rules are intended to guarantee victory to only one side: to the side that speaks up loudly to condemn sexual minority citizens. If only these opponents speak, then no balance, no final truth, can be realized. And in that unbalanced situation, the third and final stage of social movement—adoption—cannot possibly occur.

In short, silence is vital to the *denial* of safety, to the denial of the fair, equal treatment that freedom in America is supposed to provide.

When the opponents to laws protecting g/b/i/l/t citizens from discrimination in the realms of jobs, housing, and public accommodation say that seeking to be listed alongside other historically discriminated-against groups is seeking "special rights," they fail to recognize that, in fact, the only "special" rights being sought are the special "rights" the attackers themselves seek to perpetuate false stereotypes; the rights opponents demand to freely attack, to impose silence, and to harm and/or discriminate against fellow citizens simply because of unchallenged prejudiced views some people hold about them.

Coming out is the best tool we have for challenging those untrue prejudiced views. One conversation I had with an African-American person who was clearly struggling with gay rights activists wanting to be covered by non-discrimination laws illuminates the need for coming out. The woman said:

Look at me – I'm black as black can be every day everywhere I go. People can always spot me and can always discriminate against me. But you can hide—it's easy for you! Why talk about something you don't have to, when racism is automatic.

I agreed it was different for her than for me, and that neither of us should be in the binds we're in. But I added that in an odd way she had an advantage, saying,

Yes, but any time you do something great, people have to notice a person of color did a great thing, and they have to face their prejudices and perhaps even reconsider them. While any time I do something great, no one would have to give their anti-gay prejudices a thought—unless I'm out to them.

Coming out, as hard and sometimes scary as it is, is the only tool I have to directly confront the untrue myths about me/us.

What really is "special" in America is the fact that there *is* a list of historically attacked groups which now do receive legal protections in an effort to lessen attacks against them. Colonial settlers founded our nation on the special right denied them in England: the special right to choose and practice the religion of one's choice. Religious freedom is dear—it is special. From that beginning point, the list of protected groups has evolved through time. Race and sex and others have been added, slowly and painfully; the most recent addition being protection regardless of physical or mental disability.

So when lesbian, bi, gay, transgender, and intersexual people seek to be added to that same list—not any new or specially separate list— we do so to seek the *very same* (not special) legal protections other citizens already are promised. Addition to the list is a vital step toward making it safer to be open and honest about our lives, so we can have legal recourse when attacked, and so we can more safely discuss and challenge the untrue stereotypes about us.

But breaking silence can't wait for the slow wheels of social change laws. Even with the passage of such laws, change will still be slow, as with all non-discrimination law. As more of us and more of our allies choose to come out with or without such laws in place, more and more capable, fully contributing non-passing intersexual, gay, bisexual, transgender, and lesbian people will gradually allow themselves to become visible within mainstream society.

Others will become less fearful as they see people surviving and succeeding in the open. This will grant additional persons the courage to also come out and be open about themselves. The people around them—friends, acquaintances, and co-workers—will better and better comprehend that we're not a threat, and never have been. They'll come to know us for who we fully are, and will no longer fear us in return.

11. Beyond Silence

It takes courage to move beyond silence. Breaking silence—refusing to pass—will in the end hasten the passage of truly equal protection under the law.

Fortunately, there's a groundswell of people coming out in the world today, no longer letting untrue stereotypes go unchallenged. What used to entail coming out only privately to friends and family has moved to intentionally coming out to the wider world. As public figures increasingly come out, too, the groundswell gains even greater momentum as more and more people discover someone they respect or trust is supportive of g/l/b/t/i equality.

Before the mid-1980's most famous gay/lesbian/trans/inter people weren't out in the mainstream press—and often we learned of their status only after their death.

But in the latter half of the twentieth century, slowly but steadily famous people began to intentionally, proactively come out in a more public way. And now, in the early twenty-first century, public figures are choosing to come out much more readily of their own accord as they're ready.

Here's a very short list of the many: Bessie Smith, "Empress of the Blues," came out as bisexual very early in the 20th century; James Baldwin, Audrey Lourde, and Gore Vidal were out early on as writers and activists; Rene Richards came out as transgendered when playing professional tennis in the '70's; world tennis champions Billie Jean King and Martina Navritalova, and Olympic diving gold medallist Greg Louganis came out as lesbian and gay while still competing in their sports; Massachusetts U.S. Senator Barney Frank came out decades ago; decorated army medical officer Colonel Margarethe Cammer-meyer came out in the '90's (and was discharged despite being up for promotion during the Bush, senior, administration); Elton John, Holly

Near, K.D. Lang and Melissa Etheridge are well known modern music front-runners; TV comedian Ellen Degeneres came out with humor and some fun on the cover of *TIME Magazine* in 1997 ("Yep, I'm Gay"); National talk show host Rosie O'Donnell came out in an ABC interview with Dianne Sawyer in 2002; The Mayor of Paris in 2003, Bertrand Delanoë, is openly gay.

The list grows longer now-days with ever-increasing speed. Each famous person who intentionally comes out helps further undo untrue negative stereotypes. Each broadens the safety net for the next person to come out. And each is surely a positive role model for young people just entering their personal sexual orientation awareness process.

Intersexuals are only now slowly starting to enter mainstream news and g/l/b/t focus. A few intersexuals are out and lobbying for better treatment and respect (see Intersex Society of North America), and surely much more will become known as more choose to come out voluntarily to speak of their experiences.

Before today's brave new intersexual activists, the only "famous" intersexual outings were generally not of the intersexual's choosing. Most involved stories of female sports competitors discovered to have sexual anomalies. Many were denied medals, or denied the right to compete at all: i.e., discrimination against intersexual women in sports. With the advent of genetic testing, another entire group of women came under fire. Some were found to their utter surprise to be XY, and were declared "male" despite their life and physical appearance being female. Other women had an XXY genotype—and likewise had no expectation of being questioned or banished from their sport. The most famous of these may be Eva Klobukowska:

> Polish sprinter Eva Klobukowska became the first public victim of the sex chromatin test in 1967, at Kiev, USSR, at the European Cup; even after several British Athletes at that time, failed the test and were quietly counseled about their new found abnormalities. This occurred a year after passing the 'old-style gynecological examination' in 1966, when she competed at the European Cup Championships in Budapest. She was found to have an XXY karyotype (Turnbull, 1988): 'one chromosome too many to be declared a woman for the purposes of athletic competition' (Donohoe et al, 1986). After a gynecological examination, which proved to be normal, she was immediately banned from competition, and publicly humiliated all over the world, because of her extra chromosome (Ryan, 1976). A few years after Miss Klobukowska became pregnant

and gave birth to a healthy baby (Sherrow, 1996). (Guilbeault, 1998-99)

Today, the use of genetic screening in sports is being seriously questioned, and the 2002 Olympics was the first to withdraw gender verification tests to screen out intersexual women (Genel 2000). But stories like these surely give intersexuals pause about voluntarily coming out.

While public b/i/g/l/t persons coming out for themselves is a powerful tool for changing public perception, famous heterosexual allies also have the opportunity to make the world safer for everyone, of every sexual minority status. For example, Coretta Scott King, widow of civil rights leader Martin Luther King Jr. is a strong ally:

'I still hear people say that I should not be talking about the rights of lesbian and gay people and that I should stick to the issue of racial justice,' she said. 'But I hasten to remind them that Martin Luther King Jr. said, 'injustice anywhere is a threat to justice everywhere.' . . . 'I appeal to everyone who believes in Martin Luther King Jr.'s dream to make room at the table of brother- and sisterhood for lesbian and gay people,' she said. (*Reuters*, March 31, 1998)

'Homophobia is like racism and anti-Semitism and other forms of bigotry in that it seeks to dehumanize a large group of people, to deny their humanity, their dignity and personhood,' King stated. 'This sets the stage for further repression and violence that spread all too easily to victimize the next minority group.' (*Chicago Defender*, April 1, 1998, p. 1)

She voiced continued support at a speech at The Richard Stockton College of New Jersey in 2004:

The widow of Martin Luther King Jr. called gay marriage a civil rights issue, denouncing a proposed constitutional amendment that would ban it.

Constitutional amendments should be used to expand freedom, not restrict it, Coretta Scott King said Tuesday.

'Gay and lesbian people have families, and their families should have legal protection, whether by marriage or civil union,' she said. 'A constitutional amendment banning same-sex marriages is a form of gay bashing and it would do nothing at all to protect traditional marriages.' (*USA Today*, March 24, 2004)

Coretta Scott King reminds us all, "the great promise of American democracy is that no group of people will be forced to suffer discrimination and injustice," (King, 1994).

The positive ripple effects of moving beyond passing can't always be predicted. Sometimes a person becomes a famous advocate without setting out to do so. By simply being out in their private life, they end up a symbol inspiring innumerable others to be more open and respectful of g/l/b/t/i persons.

For example, when terrorists hijacked the passenger planes on September 11, 2001, that hit the Pentagon and New York's Twin Towers, gay rugby player Mark Bingham was one of the passengers on board Flight 93 who fought with the hijackers for control of the plane. Flight 93 crashed in a Pennsylvania field during the struggle killing all aboard, but not hitting the terrorists' intended target. Bingham's partner and family wanted the world to fully understand that Mark, an American hero who died trying to save lives, was an openly out gay man (Heredia, *San Francisco Chronicle*, 2002). Because he had been out, they, too, chose not to pass and instead to come out as family and partner of a gay man so they could bring fully to life the memory of Mark Bingham. When Republican Senator John McCain (Presidential candidate in 2000) gave Mark's eulogy he said in part,

> I love my country, and I take pride in serving her. But I cannot say that I love her more or as well as Mark Bingham did, or the other heroes on United Flight 93 who gave their lives to prevent our enemies from inflicting an even greater injury on our country. It has been my fate to witness great courage and sacrifice for America's sake, but none greater than the selfless sacrifice of Mark Bingham and those good men who grasped the gravity of the moment, understood the threat, and decided to fight back at the cost of their lives. . . .
>
> It is now believed that the terrorists on Flight 93 intended to crash the airplane into the United States Capitol where I work, the great house of democracy where I was that day. It is very possible that I would have been in the building, with a great many other people, when that fateful, terrible moment occurred, and a beautiful symbol of our freedom was destroyed along with hundreds if not thousands of lives. I may very well owe my life to Mark and the others who summoned the enormous courage and love necessary to deny those depraved, hateful men their terrible triumph. Such a debt you incur for life.

I will try very hard, very hard, to discharge my public duties in a manner that honors their memory. All public servants are now solemnly obliged to do all we can to help this great nation remain worthy of the sacrifice of New York City firefighters, police officers, emergency medical people, and worthy of the sacrifice of the brave passengers on Flight 93. (McCain, Eulogy, Press Release, September 22, 2001)

Because Marks' partner and family had had the courage not to pass, all of Congress knew Mark was gay, and Congress and people around the world could include "hero" in a description of a famous gay man.

In this fashion, step by step, person by person—whether famous or within personal circles of friends and family and community—surely negative stereotypes will not long endure as passing passes away.

Beyond passing—beyond silence. The ripple effects spread, and we may never know who all is affected or helped by them.

What we do know, however, with history as our guide, is that the road from any prejudice to mutual trust and safety is a long one.

Passing's role in providing safety from prejudice has had a higher price tag than most of us are aware of.

But the move beyond silence, beyond passing, will lessen everyone's fear. With the lessening of fear will surely come the lessening of the discrimination and violence against people now held hostage by society's untrue stereotypes about them.

Speaking out surely hastens the day when the safety net—the area free from pain and fear for everyone concerned—will be widened, and the lives of *everyone* will be enriched as a result.

Courage is the price that Life exacts
for granting peace.

~ Amelia Earhart, 1927

Reflections—

21. "Easy to break the silence? No. But silence can become unbearable when the price in loss of integrity finally becomes too great."

    a. Who have you come out to (as being lesbian, intersexual, gay, trans, bi, or as someone who is family, friend, or ally to someone who is)?

    b. Why did you come out to them?

    c. What was the coming out like for you? For them?

    d. Did their initial reaction evolve over time? How?

    e. How do you feel now about having come out to them?

    f. Are there other people you'd like to come out to some day? Why?

22. "Subservience, silence—neither should be the price of safety. And neither is the essence of freedom. The imposition of either means that persons suffering the oppression have fewer actual rights than other citizens."

    a. Imagine American's struggle for integration if opponents of integration had intimidated supporters into silence: no marches, no testimony, no letters, and no speeches.

    b. Consider other ways in which other groups of people "come out." What if a variety of groups were forced *not* to come out, and were promised no harm would come to them *only* if they kept their secret? (Examples: what if religious persons were barred from wearing a cross, a Star of David, or from saying "I am a Jew" or "I am a Christian." Or married people were forcibly kept from wearing a wedding ring. Or heterosexuals couldn't put their opposite-gender partner's picture on their desk or discuss their dates, wear engagement rings, or announce marriage plans.)

Imagine saying to people in these and other groups that they must keep their group membership secret or suffer "justified" discrimination.

23. "When opponents to laws protecting g/b/i/l/t citizens from discrimination in the realms of jobs, housing, education say that seeking to be listed alongside other discriminated-against groups is seeking 'special rights,' they fail to recognize that, in fact, the only 'special' rights being sought are the special 'rights' the attackers themselves seek to perpetuate false stereotypes . . . ."

   a. Current laws protect people from job, housing, and public accommodation discrimination on the basis of many listed statuses, among them race, religion, color, national origin, sex/gender, age, marital status, changes in marital status, parental status, veteran status, mental, and physical disability. Do you think any of these status(es) were seeking "special rights" when struggling to be added to the list?

   b. Involvement in certain of the above legally protected groups is a matter of choice or is invisible enough to enable successful passing. Since people could change their status to avoid certain prejudices (examples: change to a non-attacked religion, not get divorced), or could keep silent about their status (not reveal a mental disability, veteran status, parental status, religion), should these statuses be removed from the protection list?

   c. Did you know that as of 2004, there are still no federal laws preventing discrimination on the basis of sexual orientation or gender identity/behavior? Did you know that because of this, transgender, gay, lesbian, intersexual, and bisexual people can be discriminated against in employment, housing, and public accommodations without any legal recourse? For that matter, since the term "sexual orientation" includes heterosexual orientation, did you know that without such federal laws, it's also perfectly legal to discriminate against people because they're *hetero*sexual (straight), too?

24. "Before the mid-1980's most famous gay/lesbian/trans/inter/bi people weren't out in the mainstream press, and often we learned of their status only after their death."

    a. Try an internet search under "famous homosexuals." Did you know there were so many? And of course the list can't be complete since there's no way to verify the sexual orientation of *everyone* from decades or centuries ago. Some on the list may well be bisexual, of course, because often any same-gender relationships long ago set people only into a "homosexual" category. Are you surprised to find out about some of them? If so why do you think you're surprised to find they're gay or lesbian (or bi)?

    b. Try an internet search under "famous bisexual." Did you know of their lives? And of course the list can't be complete since there's no way to verify the sexual orientation of *everyone* from decades or centuries ago. Are you surprised to find out about some of them? If so why do you think you're surprised to find they're bisexual?

    c. Try an internet search under "famous transgender" or "famous transsexual." Did you know about their lives? Again, the list can't be complete since there's no way to verify the gender status of *everyone* from decades or centuries ago. Are you surprised to find out about some of them? If so why do you think you're surprised to find they're transgender?

    d. Try an internet search under "famous intersexual." You'll notice not as much is available yet, because intersexuals have only begun to come out relatively recently. But of course the list can't be complete since there's no way to verify the gender variations of *everyone* from decades or centuries ago. Here's one example, just for a start:

> Poised to cast the deciding vote in a Salisbury, Connecticut, election in 1843, 'Levi S.' was charged with being a woman and therefore ineligible. A doctor found that Levi also had a vagina and menstruated regularly. What to do? Today we may be amused at 19th century conundrums concerning an intersexual person in a society in which only men held the

right to vote. But modern America still requires citizens to be either male or female . . . . (Breedlove, reviewing the book *Sexing the Body: Gender Politics and the Construction of Sexuality.* By Anne Fausto-Sterling, 2000.)

e. Try an internet search under "famous berdache." This is an anthropological term for Native Americans who were inter-sexual, transgender, or non-heterosexual. Before European sup-pression of Native culture, the berdache, considered a third male-female gender, were often a tribe's honored leaders or shamans, believed to be a valuable link between male and female spirits. Here's one search result:

> Perhaps the most famous berdache was We'wha from the Zuni tribe of New Mexico. (The Zuni call people of inter-mediate gender lhamana.) We'wha, who was physically male but dressed as a female, was a key representative of Native tribes in the 1880s. She traveled to Washington to speak with then President, Grover Cleveland, and other delegates.
>
> Many were impressed by the six-foot tall woman, who had the refined sense of a princess and the strength of a warrior. Interestingly, the president never learned that she was physically a man until years after the visit. Many photos of We'wha still exist, and her story has been documented in books and more recently on the Internet. (Fleer, *Imprint Online: Human* - Friday, May 19, 2000.Volume 23, Number 2).

f. Do an internet search under "two-spirited." Here's one search result:

> The Two-spirited person is a native [American] tradition that anthropologists have been able to date to some of the earliest discoveries of Native artifacts. Much evidence indicates that Native [American] people, prior to colo-nization and contact with European cultures, believed in the existence of three genders: the male, the female and the male-female gender, or what we now call the Two-spirited person. The term Two-spirited, though relatively new, was derived from interpretations of Native languages used to describe people who displayed both characteristics of male and female.

Traditionally, the Two-spirited person was one who had received a gift from the Creator, that gift being the privilege to house both male and female spirits in their bodies. The concept of Two-spirited related to today's designation of gays, lesbians, bisexual and transgender persons of Native origins [and quite probably intersexual persons as well]. Being given the gift of two-spirits meant that this individual had the ability to see the world from two perspectives at the same time. This greater vision was a gift to be shared with all, and as such, Two-spirited beings were revered as leaders, mediators, teachers, artists, seers, and spiritual guides. They were treated with the greatest respect, and held important spiritual and ceremonial responsibilities. (Project/ Project Interaction, McGill University)

g. Why do you think this information (lists of historic figures who were homosexual, bisexual, transgender, or intersexual) isn't general public knowledge? Do you think it should be? What might be gained if it were?

12. Everyone Can Come Out, A-Z:
Ideas for straight allies, and for gay, lesbian, bisexual, transgender, and intersexual people

Coming out—breaking silence—as a sexual minority person or as an ally for people who are, is the best tool there is for ending the untrue myths and stereotypes that silence has held in place for too long.

Courageously speaking out and sharing our stories is the ultimate antidote for ending the personal and societal pain that pressure to pass as always/only traditionally heterosexual has historically imposed.

Not to say coming out is easy. It usually isn't. But it can be exhilarating. In my experience, at its essence coming out is both freeing and healing at a deep inner soul level where I believe we all desire to be seen and known, and if not accepted, then at least understood.

Ideas for coming out:

a. Number one rule: trust your intuition. You decide when, how, and to whom to come out.

b. Rule number two: there are no more rules. Every person steps out in his or her own style. Experiment with people you love and trust, and learn from each experience. Ask other people how they've come out as g/l/b/t/i or as people who love and support us. Read books about others' experiences. Parents, Families and Friends of Lesbians and Gays (PFLAG) has good booklets, audio tapes and videos at low cost, plus an excellent book reading list. (See the *Contact Information* section for more on PFLAG and other supportive organizations.) The following are some ideas, things that have worked for me and for others. Try them and/or create you own steps.

c.   Have a "coming out stories" party and invite supportive family, friends, and allies of bi, gay, transgender, lesbian, and intersexual people. Tell each other your coming-to-terms and coming out stories. Remember to keep it personal: you're coming out for yourself. If you're g/l/b/t/i, this is your chance to talk about your own experiences in a safe and welcoming environment. If you're coming out as a supporter of g/l/b/t/i people, remember not to use your friend or loved one's name unless you have their permission to do so. Just saying "I have a friend" or "I have a relative who is" is enough. Laugh, cry, and learn from each other—and brainstorm about how to open up with more people about your status or about your support for those you care about.

d.   Write in a journal about your coming out fears. What's the worst that could happen? What's the best that could happen? How does the status quo feel? Whom do you want to come out to? Why?

e.   Write a coming out letter or make a coming out phone call to someone you care about. Let them know about you. And let them know you're supportive of equal rights and fair treatment of everyone regardless of sexual orientation or gender identity/behavior/status. Remember, you're coming out *for yourself:* don't use your friend or loved one's name unless you have their permission to do so. Follow up with another letter, phone call or visit. Share your coming out stories with your l/g/b/t/i friends and fellow allies.

f.   Set up the time and place and setting for an optimal face to face coming out environment for someone important in your life.

g.   Be there to support your friends who have hard times with friends or family or co-workers that don't react well to coming out news. Seek support if you have a hard time. Remember that many times a friend or family's initial negative reaction can evolve into acceptance. Be patient. Remember, you didn't change anything except your level of openness and honesty. Remind them you told them because you care about them. Acknowledge their struggle to incorporate the news. Share your struggle to keep silent.

h. Join a PFLAG group or start one. Support is a wonderful thing; you're not alone, and having others to talk to can make a world of difference.

i. Have good written material ready to give or loan friends and family who want or need more information after you come out to them. Parents, Families and Friends of Lesbians and Gays (PFLAG) has good booklets, audio tapes, and videos at low cost, and an excellent book reading list. Some other good resources include the Intersex Society of North America (ISNA); the Bisexual Resource Center; and the International Foundation for Gender Education. (See the *Contact Information* section for more on all these groups.)

j. Mourn any lost friends or family ties that coming out causes. Remember: you valued the relationship enough to give it your all. Respect your courage, heal your heart, and seek out friends and loved ones who do value the *total* you!

k. Celebrate your successes!

l. Insert occasional low-key lesbian/gay/trans/inter positive comments into everyday conversation. The words and topic need not always be "charged." For example, if discussion is going on about a topic and there's an unspoken non-heterosexual element to it, feel free to bring it up. Examples are endless, but here are a few: If someone's saying they like Elton John's latest song, say something like, "It sounds like he's relieved to have come out as being gay. I like his music too. My favorite song of his is 'x.'" Or, when gays in the military comes up, say something like, "Isn't it something that a 1992 Soldier of the Year turned out to be gay?" [28]
     Also, careful use of humor can be fun. My mom recently told a story about me to a group of friends. She told them I'd recently reroofed their house, and had pointed to the roof proudly and said, "Those shingles are pretty darned straight for me not being straight!"

m. Interrupt stereotype "jokes" and anti-g/l/b/t/i discussions. This can be done in a very non-confrontive way, and can be done likewise to interrupt negative comments about any other group as well (disability, sexist, racist, etc.). Personalize your comments so you don't have to get caught up in attacking the person who made the inappropriate remark. Just let them know it hurt you and you don't like hearing it. To do this, you can calmly say things like (insert any group—here it's for non-heterosexuals):

-   I know gay people who don't fit that stereotype at all. That joke doesn't seem funny to me.
-   I'd appreciate it if you didn't tell lesbian jokes around me. I know and care about some people that are lesbian and gay, and it hurts to hear comments like that.
-   I know and respect someone who's bisexual. If you knew my friend, you wouldn't believe stories like that.
-   You know, no one gets to choose their particular body. I know people who feel they just got dealt the wrong one as far as gender goes, and that can't be easy! I'd appreciate not hearing negative comments about them around me. Thanks.

n. Challenge the untrue stereotypes about us every chance you get, every way you can. It's the *stereotype* that frightens people. Coming out as a sexual minority person or as someone who supports us provides the most concrete proof possible that the stereotype is a lie.

o. Every October 11 is "National Coming Out Day." It marks the anniversary of the 1987 "March on Washington" for lesbian/gay/bi/transgender rights. Plan ahead and come out to a friend or family member each October 11th. Attend a local coming out event. Create one if none is planned.

p. Come out as a supporter of our equal rights. If necessary, you can do so without coming out personally. Broad coalitions are working together everywhere for laws and policies that don't discriminate against us. You can join the many people of all sexual orientations who support sexual minority issues, *without* having to identify your own personal connection. For example you can write a letter supporting a b/l/g/i/t- positive political issue. Send it to your congress members, counsel members, legislators, or school board.

q. Do #17 above, but do come out personally. Say, "I'm gay, and here's what it's like for me and people I know," or say "I know and love someone who's bisexual, and here's what it's like for me and for people I know and care about." If you have your family or friend's permission, you can personalize it more by saying, "My daughter is a lesbian, and I love her very much. The stereotypes used to attack all homosexuals are just not true."

r. Write a letter to the editor of your local paper to correct mis-information that anti-gay or gay-ignorant people submit. Once again, you can come out as a supporter/ally for the issue or personally. Either way is invaluable in the scope of balancing public debate.

    Or write a positive letter to the editor totally separate from any negative press. We need not always play catch-up to negative comments others have written. We can create our own positive press!

s. Wear a pin with poet Audre Lorde's words, "Your Silence Will Not Protect You:" a good self-reminder. Or wear a "Straight But Not Narrow" pin: a great conversation starter.

t. Wear a pink or black triangle pin. (The Nazis made gay men wear pink triangles and made lesbians wear black triangles. Books and magazines speaking positively of homosexuals were among the first censored and burned by the Nazis, and many homosexuals were sent to the concentration camps).

u. Go to a Pride Month event. June is national Pride Month in honor of the 1969 Stonewall riots in New York, where patrons of a gay bar fought back against police intent on raiding the establishment. Stonewall is considered by many to be the start of the g/l/b/t American civil rights movement.

v. Accept an invitation to attend a friend or family member's same-gender marriage, civil union, or other solemnization of relationship ceremony. And/or send an anniversary card to a same-sex couple that is out to you.

w. Vote! And encourage others to vote too; get politically involved:

Vote for and support only those candidates who support g/l/b/t/i full equal rights.

Actively support legalizing civil marriage for same-sex couples whenever the opportunity arises. Speak positively of extending *all* federal and state benefits/responsibilities of marriage to same-sex couples via marriage (or civil unions) every chance you get.

And just as actively oppose any federal or state constitutional amendment to ban civil marriage for same-sex couples. Educate everyone you know that the constitution is for *giving* citizens rights, not taking rights away.

x. Actively support legalizing adoption and foster parenting by same-gender couples whenever the opportunity arises. Speak positively of both in every setting you can. Vote for supportive candidates.

y. Attend a local, state or national march for our rights. It's a life-changing experience to march publicly in a large group, demanding the American basics of safety, respect, and equality.

And attend local, state, or national marches for *everyone's* rights, those which specifically include protection for sexual orientation and gender identity/behavior/status along with protection for every other group. Bigotry is bigotry. Stand up for others' rights as they stand up for yours. Bi, intersexual, transgender, lesbian, and gay people—and out allies—exist in *every* group, of every political party, language, economic situation, marital or parental status, religion, ability, race, sex, age, ethnicity, or national origin. We are them and they are us! Building and cherishing these coalitions of support will make it safer, over time, for everyone to be more fully themselves.

z. Send money and/or volunteer time to organizations that work for equal rights and fair treatment regardless of sexual orientation, gender expression and identity, or gender status. Not everyone can be an activist, but we can support the ones who are!

Congratulate yourself for doing any of the above, and for any other ideas you develop. Your effort and integrity have made the safety net broader and the world a safer place for you and countless other people.

Cautious, careful people,
always casting about to preserve
their reputation and social standing,
never can bring about a reform.
Those who are really in earnest
must be willing to be anything
or nothing in the world's estimation,
and publicly and privately in season
and out, avow their sympathies with
despised and persecuted ideas and their
advocates, and bear the consequences.

~ Susan B. Anthony

Contact Information

Parents, Families and Friends of Lesbians & Gays (PFLAG)

http://www.pflag.org/

PFLAG is a national organization begun in 1981 by parents of gay and lesbian children. It has a newspaper and a comprehensive list of books, articles, cassettes and video tapes designed for understanding homosexual, bisexual, transgender and intersexual persons' lives. People of all sexual orientations are welcome to join, and to benefit from the organization's many resources.

Excerpts from http://www.pflag.org/):

PFLAG's Vision

We, the parents, families and friends of lesbian, gay, bisexual and transgendered persons, celebrate diversity and envision a society that embraces everyone, including those of diverse sexual orientations and gender identities. Only with respect, dignity and equality for all will we reach our full potential as human beings, individually and collectively. PFLAG welcomes the participation and support of all who share in, and hope to realize this vision.

PFLAG's Mission

PFLAG promotes the health and well-being of gay, lesbian, bisexual and transgendered persons, their families and friends through: support, to cope with an adverse society; education, to enlighten an ill-informed public; and advocacy, to end discrimination and to secure equal civil rights. Parents, Families and Friends of Lesbians and Gays provides opportunity for dialogue about sexual orientation and gender identity, and acts to create a society that is healthy and respectful of human diversity.

Support For Gay, Lesbian, Bisexual or Transgendered People:

PFLAG is a home for gay, lesbian, bisexual and transgendered people. We understand, and we offer our support and unconditional love.

Being gay, lesbian, bisexual or transgendered is a normal and healthy way to be. Your sexual orientation and gender identity are just one more part of who you are. And sometimes, it takes time to know who you are. It is okay to be confused, it's okay to be unsure whether you are gay or straight and to be uncertain about whether you should come out. Remember, you are not alone. There are people out there with the same questions and concerns that you have. And there are people who have already found their own answers. PFLAG is here to help you find your own answers.

Every day, all across the country, PFLAG is working to help keep families together. PFLAG support group meetings provide a safe space for gay, lesbian, bisexual, transgendered and questioning people to share their feelings and experiences, to explore their identity, and to seek the acceptance and unconditional love that our members have to offer. Sometimes, it just helps to have someone to talk to. PFLAG has chapters in over 460 communities all have help-lines you can call. We can help you find a chapter near you.

PFLAG also supports, educates and advocates for equal civil rights for gay, lesbian, bisexual and transgendered people and invites all people who share our vision to join us in our work.

PFLAG's 2002 Intersexuality Policy:

At least one in 2000 children is born with notably atypical sexual anatomy, i.e., an intersex condition. In our culture, sexual variation which blurs the line between male and female is stigmatized. The presence of a genital anomaly often elicits feelings of guilt and shame.

PFLAG supports efforts to end the secrecy and the medically unnecessary genital surgery experienced by some intersex persons. PFLAG welcomes the efforts of medical organizations, support groups, and others, working toward this end. PFLAG urges the entire medical community to establish and adopt a patient-centered treatment protocol under which patients are treated with the utmost sensitivity. Full and accurate information should be disclosed to parents of newborn intersex children, and appropriate referrals, including to support groups of adult intersex people, should be provided.

PFLAG encourages its members to be sensitive to the needs of intersex persons and their families as they address societal issues and biases which contribute to their shame, guilt, and isolation.

PFLAG welcomes intersex persons and their families as fully participating members.

Adopted by the PFLAG Board of Directors
on September 27, 2002.

PFLAG's recommended reading list is available online at
http://www.pflag.org/publications/recommended_reading.pdf

For information about the nearest PFLAG chapter or help-line in the United States or Canada, call 202-467-8180 (voice); 202-638-0243 (fax); Email: info@pflag.org; Homepage: www.pflag.org/. Mail to: PFLAG, 1726 M St. NW, Suite 400, Washington, DC 20036, USA.

Bisexual Resource Center, serving the bisexual community since 1985

Excerpts from http://www.biresource.org/:

Bisexual Resource Center's 2003 Mission Statement:

We envision a world where everyone's love is celebrated, regardless of gender(s). We believe in a world that acknowledges people as whole and indivisible and where they should not have to leave any part of their heritage and identity at the door. Oppression on the basis of sexual identity is intertwined with all other oppressions.

The Bisexual Resource Center is a non-profit 501(c)(3) educational organization incorporated in the Commonwealth of Massachusetts as the 'East Coast Bisexual Network, Inc.' The purposes of the corporation are:

• To research and educate the general public and other interested organizations about bisexuality;

• To provide a public forum through technical assistance, seminars, conferences, informational programs and publications for the discussion of bisexuality;

• To provide a support network for individual members of the general public and interested organizations to discuss and obtain information about bisexuality; and

• To act exclusively for educational and charitable purposes as defined under section 501(c)(3) of the Internal Revenue Code of 1954 (or the corresponding provision of any future United States Internal Revenue Law).

The Bisexual Resource Center also has publications, including the following:

The all-new, up-to-date *Bisexual Resource Guide 4th Edition*:

From the preface:

Listing 352 bi groups and 2129 bi-inclusive groups in 66 countries, as well as bibliographies, film guides and some awesome quotes and photos, the Bisexual Resource Guide, 4th Edition is evidence that the bi movement has indeed come a long way. The growth in the number of bi groups over the years is evidence of a burgeoning movement, but perhaps even more powerful a statement is the number of groups which formerly ignored (or even denied access to) bisexual people which now include us. This expansion of 'community' is a continuing international trend, and it will help to make it easier for bisexual people to identify as such, and easier for all of us—lesbian, gay, bisexual, heterosexual, transgendered, intersexed, queer, and questioning—to find comfort with ourselves and a sense of community with others, even if and when our identities change over our lifetimes.

For more information contact the Bisexual Resource Center at: 617/424-9595 (v), or postal mail to: Bisexual Resource Center, PO Box 1026, Boston, MA 02117-1026, USA.

Website http://www.biresource.org/; email brc@biresource.org.

Transgender: The International Foundation for Gender Education

Here is one internet group; there are many more online.
Excerpts from www.ifge.org/:

The International Foundation for
Gender Education
www.ifge.org

The International Foundation for Gender Education (IFGE), founded in 1987, is a leading advocate and educational organization for promoting the self-definition and free expression of individual gender identity. IFGE is not a support group, it is an information provider and clearinghouse for referrals about all things which are transgressive of established social gender norms. IFGE maintains the most complete bookstore on the subject of transgenderism available anywhere. It also publishes the leading magazine providing reasoned discussion of issues of gender expression and identity, including crossdressing, transsexualism, FTM [female to male] and MTF [male to female] issues spanning health, family, medical, legal, workplace issues and more.

IFGE values:
• individual uniqueness and dignity;
• personal wholeness;
• respect for human diversity;
• freedom from society's arbitrarily assigned gender definitions;
• respect, acceptance, enforcement, and protection of gender-related Human and Civil Rights for all.

Mailing address: IFGE, P.O. Box 540229, Waltham, MA 02454-0229. USA. Voice: 781-894-8340 or 781-899-2212Fax: 781-899-5703. Email: info@ifge.org

Intersex Society of North America

Excerpts from ISNA, http://www.isna.org/, in 2003:

The Intersex Society of North America is devoted to systemic change to end shame, secrecy, and unwanted genital surgeries for people born with an anatomy that someone decided is not standard for male or female. We urge physicians to use a model of care that is patient-centered, rather than concealment-centered:

- Intersexuality is basically a problem of stigma and trauma, not gender.
- Parents' distress must not be treated by surgery on the child.
- Professional mental health care is essential.
- Honest, complete disclosure is good medicine.
- All children should be assigned as boy or girl, without early surgery.

ISNA's Recommendations for Treatment:
http://www.isna.org/library/recommendations.html

© 1994 Intersex Society of North America
PO Box 301 Petaluma CA 94953 email: info@isna.org

Why this document?
  The current model of treatment for intersexual infants and children, established in the 1950's, asserts that since the human species is sexually dimorphic, all humans must appear to be either exclusively male or female, and that children with visibly intersexual anatomy cannot develop into healthy adults. The model therefore recommends emergency sex assignment and reinforcement in the sex of assignment with early genital surgery. It also encourages care providers to be less than honest with parents and with intersexuals about their true status.
  As a growing number of us who are intersexual have shared our experiences with each other, we have reached the conclusion that, for

most of us, this management model has led to profoundly harmful sorts of medical intervention and to neglect of badly needed emotional support. Our intersexuality—our status as individuals who are neither typical males nor typical females—is not beneficially altered by such treatment. Instead, it is pushed out of the view of parents and care providers. This 'conspiracy of silence'—the policy of pretending that our intersexuality has been medically eliminated—in fact simply exacerbates the predicament of the intersexual adolescent or young adult who knows that s/he is different, whose genitals have often been mutilated by 'reconstructive' surgery, whose sexual functioning has been severely impaired, and whose treatment history has made clear that acknowledgment or discussion of our intersexuality violates a cultural and a family taboo.

What is the Intersex Society?

The Intersex Society of North America (ISNA) is a peer support, education, and advocacy group founded and operated by and for intersexuals. We are pleased to have the assistance and counsel of three professional sexologists who serve on our Board of Directors.

A new model of treatment:

Based on discussions with dozens of adult intersexuals, we are prepared to recommend a new paradigm for the management of intersexual children. Our model is based upon avoidance of harmful or unnecessary surgery, qualified professional mental health care for the intersexual child and his/her family, and empowering the intersexual to understand his/her own status and to choose (or reject) any medical intervention.

ISNA—Building a world free of shame, secrecy,
and unwanted sexual surgeries

Straight Spouse Network

Excerpts from <u>www.ssnetwk.org/</u>:

Welcome to the Straight Spouse Network (SSN), formerly Straight Spouse Support Network. SSN is an international support network of heterosexual spouses and partners, current or former, of gay, lesbian, bisexual, and transgender mates. Members provide confidential personal support and resource information to spouses and partners nationwide and abroad. SSN is the only support network of its kind in the world.

As outreach, the network offers information about spouse and family issues, mixed orientation marriages and spouse resources to professionals, community organizations and the media.

- over 65 support groups across the United States
- spouse contacts for individual sharing in every state and eight foreign countries
- eight online support groups, most with chats and webs attached
- strictly nonprofit funded by tax deductible donations
- funded by tax deductible donations

Ten Years and Still Growing!

2002 marks the tenth year that the Straight Spouse Network has been helping spouses and partners!

Our Mission:

- Reaching Out—To expand the visibility of straight spouses and extend access to support for straight spouses and partners, current or former, of gay, lesbian, bisexual, or transgender mates world wide.
- Healing—To expand support resources for spouses and partners that lessen their trauma, help them to cope with painful issues constructively, and nurture their strength to rebuild their lives.

> • Building Bridges—To foster understanding between spouses or partners and in families, and to work with community and professional organizations toward improving services for spouses.

E-Mail: dir@ssnetwk.org. Web: www.ssnetwk.org/ Postal Mail: Straight Spouse Network (SSN), Amity Pierce Buxton, Ph.D., 8215 Terrace Drive, El Cerrito, CA 94530-3058. Telephone: (510) 525-0200.

Endnotes

[1] *Sexual Orientation:* is about who you're attracted to, who you're oriented toward being sexual with.

If you realize you're attracted to the opposite gender, then your orientation is considered heterosexual. If you realize you're attracted to the same gender, then your orientation is gay or lesbian (or homosexual). If you're attracted to both the same and the opposite gender (to both men and women), then your orientation is bisexual.

Research shows sexual orientation is on a continuum from strictly heterosexual to strictly homosexual, with between thirty-three and fifty percent of people falling somewhere between the two when viewing their life in its entirety (Reinisch with Beasley, 1990, pp. 139-140, 142). Over an entire lifetime, a person may have one or two attractions or relationships outside their overall norm; others may move along the continuum of orientation as they only belatedly begin to more clearly realize their orientation.

An example is a person who for much of their life believes themselves to be heterosexual, only to fall in love with someone of the same gender later in life and realize belatedly they're actually bisexual—or perhaps even gay or lesbian. Or a person who believed themselves to be gay or lesbian who falls in love with a same-gender person and realizes belatedly they're bisexual.

As discussed at length in Part Two, orientation precedes and is separate from behavior. One can be gay in orientation (meaning one is physically and emotionally attracted to same-gender persons) but choose to behave heterosexually. Or vice versa. But that doesn't mean one's orientation has changed. It simply means a person is not behaving true to their orientation.

Of course "simply" is not the best word: try to imagine making an intimate relationship with someone you're not attracted to. So-called "conversion therapy" would try to have people be sexually and emotionally intimate with people they're not attracted to (or be celibate). But even if behavior is modified, it's only a chosen behavior at odds with one's innate orientation. It's not a change in one's internal orientation/attractions.

2   *Gender:* The term "gender" is used in most cases where the term "sex" may have been used in years past.

Today, in many circles, "gender" has taken on a broader, more inclusive meaning than "sex" generally brings to mind. Gender is meant to imply *everything* every person is—their thoughts, actions, desires, hobbies, roles, and aspirations—everything a man or woman is in their *entirety*—without sexual behavior as a limiting focus.

In lesbian, bi, gay, and transgender circles, the term gender is often preferred to underscore that our lives are vastly larger than the sexual aspect we are too often forced to defend and/or suffer for. For better or for worse, the word "sex" can shift people into limited preconceptions that can be detrimental to unbiased clear communication, empathy, and understanding.

For this reason, the term gender has been welcomed to ease the journey toward meeting one another on common ground.

3   *Bisexual* (or bi): The following is an excerpt from the Bisexual Resource Center's pamphlet "Bisexuality." It (and other information) can be ordered from: Bisexual Resource Center, Box 1026 Boston, MA 02117, USA. Phone 617-424-9595; http://www.biresource.org.

> *What is Bisexuality?* Bisexuality is the potential to feel sexually attracted to and to engage in sensual or sexual relationships with people of either sex. A bisexual person may not be equally attracted to both sexes, and the degree of attraction may vary over time.
>
> Self-perception is the key to a bisexual identity. Many people engage in sexual activity with people of both sexes, yet do not identify as bisexual. Likewise, other people engage in sexual relations only with people of one sex, or do not engage in sexual activity at all, yet consider themselves bisexual. There is no behavioral 'test' to determine whether or not one is bisexual. . . . .
>
> *Bisexual Relationships:* Bisexuals, like all people, have a wide variety of relationship styles. Contrary to common myth, a bisexual person does not need to be sexually involved with both a man and a woman simultaneously. In fact, some people who identify as bisexual never engage in sexual activity with one or the other (or either) gender. As is the case for heterosexuals and gay men and lesbians, attraction does not involve acting on every desire. Like heterosexuals and gay people, many bisexuals choose to be sexually active with one partner only, and have long-term, monogamous relationships. Other bisexuals may have open marriages that allow for relationships with same-sex partners, three-way relationships, or a number of partners of the same or other gender (singly or simultaneously). It is important to have the freedom to choose the type

of sexual and affectional relationships that are right for the people involved, whatever their sexual orientation. (Bisexual Resource Center's pamphlet 'Bisexuality,' at http://www.biresource.org/)

4   *Transgender* (or transsexual, or trans) persons challenge society's traditional view that gender is fixed. Instead, all cultural training to the contrary, in fact not everyone believes their body's birth-gender is right for them. Many choose to live as the opposite gender with or without changing their physical body via hormonal and/or surgical means. Their sexual orientation is as varied as non-transgendered persons: many transgendered people are heterosexual; some are lesbian, gay, or bisexual.

Not long ago, information about transgender persons was relatively scant. But now, information is more readily available. An example of a mainstream press article was the July 18, 1994 *New Yorker* piece titled "The Body Lies" by Amy Bloom. In it she wrote:

> Approximately two people in every hundred thousand are diagnosed (first by themselves, then by endocrinologists, family doctors, psychiatrists, or psychologists) as high-intensity transsexuals, meaning they will be motivated, whether or not they succeed, to have the surgery that will bring their bodies into accord with the gender that they have known themselves, from toddlerhood, to be. Until ten years ago, the clinical literature and the notoriously unreliable statistics suggested that for every four men seeking to become anatomically female, there was one woman seeking the opposite. Now clinical-evaluations centers report the ratio as almost one to one. (38)

For more information, there are a number of books, periodical articles, and perhaps most increasingly prevalent, Internet Web sites too numerous to list.

5   *Intersexual* (inter): Intersex persons challenge society's traditional view that gender is singular and certain. "Intersexuals are individuals born with anatomy or physiology which differ from cultural ideals of male or female" (Intersex Society of North America, ISNA: http://www.isna.org/):

> [Intersexual] frequency may be as high as 2% of live births. The frequency of individuals receiving 'corrective' genital surgery, however, probably runs between 1 and 2 per 1,000 live births (0.1-0.2%). [Abstract of 'How sexually dimorphic are we?' Review and synthesis by Melanie Blackless, Anthony Charuvastra, Amanda Derryck, Anne Fausto-Sterling, Karl Lauzanne, Ellen Lee. American Journal of Human Biology 12:151-166, 2000. © 2000 Wiley-Liss, Inc.]

The western medical model established in the 1950's asserted that children with visibly unusual or ambiguous genitalia would be unable to grow to healthy adulthood. Western medicine's recommended solution: "sex assignment and reinforcement in the sex of assignment with early genital surgery" (ISNA). The medical goal: to alter a child's external genitals "so that the child will grow up appearing to be a 'normal' male or female. . . . In about 90% of the cases, intersex infants undergo genital surgery to make them appear as a 'normal' female" (Robinson).

Other intersexuals don't display external anomalies until puberty—and some never do. For some individuals, an outwardly visible male may actually have an XX genotype; and some outwardly visible females may be XY. In addition, both self-identified males and females may in fact be XXY—and many are not aware of their intersexual status until adulthood. In fact, all through their lives many intersexuals are kept in the dark about their intersexuality even when they undergo medical intervention. Parents and/or the medical profession withhold the true reason for various procedures in an effort to enforce one unquestioned gender upon the intersexual person, despite the intersexual's frequent awareness of feeling different. This leaves many intersexuals in a very isolated state of angst. For two examples:

> In her late twenties when trying to ascertain the details of her own anatomy from her physicians, Sarah said, 'And they wouldn't tell me anything. I knew there was more to it than all this . . . . I knew that I wasn't being told the truth but there was no way anybody was gonna tell me the truth. It was such a mess. There was so much lying and symboling going on that there's a wonder I ever figured it out.'
>   . . . [and] According to Max, 'Intersexuals aren't encouraged to be autonomous, period. I mean, who we are is dictated to us. That's been my experience. And that's why I had no identity and I struggled so hard to find one.' (Preves, p. 56)

Other people might never realize they have an intersexual condition because their bodies appear and function as one gender only. For these intersexuals-unaware, their intersexual status may only come to light "when they attend a fertility treatment clinic in later life as they struggle to have their own children." (Mollenkott, quoting Whittle, 2001, p. 45)

Regarding sexual orientation, intersexuals, too, are as varied as any other group: many are heterosexual; some are bisexual, gay, or lesbian.

Today, a growing number of intersexual adults who underwent surgeries as infants and young children are questioning the medical "sexual assignment" model. Concerns such as informed consent, self-determination, and honest discussion about the potential damage to erotic function that can result from surgical intervention are coming to the fore. As is the recognition that peer support and positive counseling are vitally important for intersexuals and their families. For example, the Intersex

Society of North America, http://www.isna.org/, proposes a new model of treatment:

> Based on discussions with dozens of adult intersexuals, we are prepared to recommend a new paradigm for the management of intersexual children. Our model is based upon avoidance of harmful or unnecessary surgery, qualified professional mental health care for the intersexual child and his/her family, and empowering the intersexual to understand his/her own status and to choose (or reject) any medical intervention. (ISNA)

6   This information was presented in a workshop in 1990 in Juneau, Alaska, by Wayne V. Pawlowski, a trainer from the national office of Planned Parenthood. The several-day workshop was titled "Understanding Sexuality in Our Society." His coverage of the sexual development of children included *all* children—including research about those who were or who thought they might be gay, bi, or lesbian. The workshop was co-sponsored by the Alaska Department of Education and the federal Alaska Cooperative Extension Service. Teachers, professional social workers, counselors and administrators from throughout Southeast Alaska attended.

7   Often, too, even just the word "homosexual" is used in the pejorative, intended to frighten or insult listeners. By tone and context it can be used to stir up scary stereotypes and to emphasize the "sex" aspect of a person's life. So, as with the term "gender," many individuals prefer the terms gay, lesbian, transgender, "bi", and "trans" to the words homosexual, bisexual, or transsexual, in an effort to allow room for acknowledging the full range of activities and interests in their lives without stressing the sexual element for which they're condemned.

8   This information also came from Planned Parenthood trainer Wayne V. Pawlowski's 1990 workshop titled "Understanding Sexuality in Our Society."

9   *Queer:* In many situations, queer is a harsh ant-gay epithet, intended to insult listeners and to stir up scary stereotypes of dangerous people.

     But today, the word queer is also often self-selected as a positive descriptor by many people whose orientation or bodies or relationships differ from traditional "norms." Queer isn't a fit for all persons' self-image, but when you hear it in a non-pejorative context it may be a person's way to respectfully refer to any version of non-traditional identity or experience:

> Originally a synonym for 'odd,' this word [queer] became a derogatory
> expression for gays in the 20th Century. Even though many people still
> use 'queer' as an anti-gay epithet, a movement emerged in the 1980s
> that calls itself queer. Used in this way, queer means sexually dissident,
> but not necessarily gay. Many gays, transsexuals, bisexuals and even
> heterosexuals whose sexuality doesn't fit into the cultural standard of
> monogamous heterosexual marriage have adopted the 'queer' label.
> (Wikholm, 1999.)

[10] In 1989, under the George Bush (senior) Administration, the United States
Department of Health and Human Services published the "Report of the
Secretary's Task Force on Youth Suicide," in DHHS Publication No.
(ADM)89-1623, for the Alcohol, Drug Abuse and Mental Health Admin-
istration.

It is valuable to note that when the report's chapter by Paul Gibson,
L.C.S.W., titled "Gay Male and Lesbian Youth Suicide" appeared, it was
considered too "pro gay" for the Bush Sr. administration, was pulled from
the complete report, and, as a result, had to be requested separately,
according to PFLAG. Fortunately chapters of PFLAG were able to obtain
and distribute copies of the hard-to-get report.

The message that we as gay and lesbian adults heard from this act
was, in effect, that it was better our youth die than our adults receive civil
rights and a fair reputation. But be that as it may, it's important to
remember that youth suicides often do not occur in isolation. One youth's
suicide is all any other youth may need to decide to make the attempt, too.
A gay youth's death can sadly inspire a straight youth to end his or her
life, and vice versa. All our youth are in this together. To abandon any
group is to risk the health—and life—of all.

A follow-up: By 1997 some groups, in particular those known to be
anti-gay, were protesting the Bush DHHS report's findings. They sug-
gested not enough research existed to support its conclusions, and denied
its call for alarm. Interestingly, Mr. Gibson, the author of the Bush report,
had himself encouraged more research, and hoped his report would lead to
more attention to gay/les/bi/trans youth, and to more studies about the
difficulties they face. In May of 1996 the Massachusetts Department of
Education released a report detailing the results of their random, statewide
test. It surveyed at-risk students in general, including those who identified
as gay, lesbian, bi, or questioning. Overall, the Massachusetts report supported many of Gibson's original findings, and went on to offer:

> students who have engaged in sexual contact with members of the same
> sex and/or who describe themselves as gay, lesbian, or bisexual are
> more likely to report alcohol/drug use, suicide attempts, and violence
> related threats/incidents. This supports the need for widespread imple-
> mentation of the Safe Schools Program for Gay and Lesbian Students of

the Massachusetts Department of Education which aims to create safe and supportive environments for these students.

For a copy of the 1995 Massachusetts Youth Risk Behavior Survey Results, contact the Massachusetts Department of Education.

[11] *Gender identity:* is how one perceives one's self—as male of as female—regardless of one's physical gender or chromosomal makeup.

For most people, gender identity matches one's physical birth-gender. But for some this is not so, and they recognize, often at a very early age, that they are transgender: their internal sense of gender identity doesn't match their physical birth gender. Many say it's equivalent to a birth defect: their body is not correct for their inner sense of self, for their internal gender identity. A physical male may perceive himself as female, trapped in a male's body. Or a physical female may perceive herself as male, trapped in a female body.

An intersexual's gender identity is also their internal sense of self, regardless of their body's external or chromosomal manifestation. An intersexual is born with physical and/or chromosomal properties of both genders, and/or ambiguous genitalia. Their inner sense of gender identity, as male or female, may or may not match the external gender they most appear to be, or have been surgically/hormonally altered to appear to be.

And again—gender identity is separate from sexual orientation. Orientation is about who you're sexually and emotionally attracted to. Gender identity is who you feel yourself to be, within.

[12] Oprah Winfrey TV talk show. "When your child acts like the opposite sex." September 1996.

[13] First names of friends I interviewed are pseudonyms. Even for those who are relatively "out" locally, it's quite another thing to be identified wherever a published book such as this might travel. Distant relatives, former army buddies, future potential employers, extended business connections—being suddenly out to any or all of one's extended connections is a sobering thought. There are so many ways in which life at home or work, now or in the future, could be made unexpectedly difficult by a revelation of one's non-majority orientation. Self-protection and self-revelation are careful, one day at a time challenges for everyone, especially on the topic of sexual orientation and gender identity/status at this current moment in history.

I'm grateful my friends shared their stories with me; this book is part of my coming out process, not theirs. I respect their right to come out when and as they choose. And I do dearly hope their stories and this book make it safer for multitudes of people to come out for themselves, more than ever before, more safely than ever before, sooner rather than later, so that these days of genuine concern can be put swiftly behind us all.

14   This is an excerpt from an editorial I wrote for Alaskan newspapers titled "Everyone Can Come Out" that was published in its entirety in the *Juneau Empire* on October 4, 1988, and in part in the *Anchorage Daily News* on October 6, 1988.

15   No federal laws exist as of 2004 to prevent people from discriminating against fellow citizens because of their real or perceived sexual orientation or gender identity/status.

While a sexual minority person is protected by federal law against discrimination on the basis of their racial or religious or disability status, and other protections offered by current civil rights laws, if someone wants instead to discriminate against them because they're bisexual, trans-gendered, lesbian, intersexual, or gay, there is no federal civil rights law to stop that from happening. Some states and some local jurisdictions have added sexual orientation and gender identity to their existing list of groups that can't be discriminated against. But most sexual minority Americans do not have even that level of protection.

The federal bill ENDA (Employment Non-Discrimination Act) was first introduced in 1994 in an effort to extend equal employment pro-tections to all citizens regardless of sexual orientation, and each year it gets more co-sponsors. It would add sexual orientation (but not yet gender identity) to the same existing list of employment equality rights that are now offered on the basis of race, religion, sex, ethnicity, disability, etc.

ENDA would not create any "special rights" list, but would simply add additional people to the already-existing job protections list.

ENDA has not yet passed Congress. Interestingly, without a law like ENDA on the books, people of every sexual orientation can be discrim-inated against legally on the basis of their orientation. This means straight (heterosexual) citizens, too, are also not protected against job discrim-ination if someone doesn't want to hire, promote, or equally com-pensate a heterosexual employee.

16   This information was provided by the Alaska Network on Domestic Vio-lence and Sexual Assault. November, 1993.

17   The Bible has long been interpreted by some as equating disability with "sin" or evil.

Historically, mental illness was often equated with being possessed by demons. Priests were not infrequently called to perform exorcisms, and people with mental disabilities suffered not just their disease, but additional injuries such as confinement to their family's home and sometimes imprisonment for being different—or even death as when they, like homosexuals, were burned at the stake during the Middle Ages.

Regarding physical disabilities, there's the story of Jesus healing a man who'd had an infirmity for almost four decades, to whom Jesus said, "See, you have been made well! Do not sin any more, so that nothing worse happens to you." But, as is so often the case, another story seems to contradict the message that disability is a punishment, as when Jesus healed a blind man and told his followers, "Neither this man nor his parents sinned."

Regardless, the societal thinking over time has often been that *someone* must have done something wrong for misfortune to happen. As with mental disabilities, people with physical disabilities, too, have often been confined to their family's home due to some form of embarrassment or even shame, as if the disability were somehow either the disabled person's or family's fault.

Supporters of the 1990 Americans with Disabilities Act had to fight generations of belief that disabled persons somehow belonged at home, out of sight and out of the mainstream. Opponents of the ADA said in effect that indeed "those people" should stay home, and accused disabled citizens of seeking "special rights" when in reality, people with disabilities, like homosexuals, were in fact only asking for the very *same* access and very same rights of participation already enjoyed by other Americans.

18   Liberace always publicly denied being gay. He even sued the *London Daily Mirror* for libel for implying that he was. But Liberace is consistently named as a famous gay man in most books on the topic. For example, the book published in 2001 written by Florida International University history professor Darden Pyron, *Liberace: an American Boy*, is certain:

> While wildly successful and good natured outwardly, Liberace, Pyron reveals, was a complicated man whose political, social and religious conservatism existed side-by-side with a lifetime of secretive homosexuality. (Amazon.com, Editorial Reviews, Synopsis)

19   When one spouse/partner in a heterosexual relationship discovers their partner is homosexual, the heterosexual (straight) partner finds themselves in a life-changing milieu of emotions. Who to talk to, what to do, how to proceed with their partner and/or on their own. And what about children and relatives?

One great resource is the book *The Other Side of the Closet: The Coming Out Crisis for Straight Spouses* by Amity Pierce Buxton, Ph.D. Another is the Straight Spouse Network (SSN), which she founded. See *Silent Lives* Contact Information section for more information, or the SSN website at www.ssnetwk.org/.

20 *Civil Union:* The following excerpt is from the "The Vermont Guide to Civil Unions," published by the Office of the Secretary of State of Vermont in 2003:

> Vermont's Civil Union law [went] into effect July 1st, 2000. This law permits eligible couples of the same sex to be joined in civil union. The eligibility criteria are discussed in this pamphlet.
> Parties to a civil union shall have all the same benefits, protections and responsibilities under Vermont law, whether they derive from statute, policy, administrative or court rule, common law or any other source of civil law, as are granted to spouses in a marriage.

21 *Domestic partnership,* or DP: many definitions of "domestic partnership" exist. Each business or health insurance company that provides domestic partner benefits establishes its own definition of what constitutes a recognized domestic partnership. Domestic partners receive some but not all of the benefits of marriage. The following from the University of Minnesota Board of Regents (1993) recommendation is a good example of a general definition:

> DEFINITION OF DOMESTIC PARTNERSHIP: This recommendation is intended to cover the relationship of same sex domestic partners and not roommates. Domestic partnership has been defined in a variety of ways by different organizations, but a certain common thread runs through all of the definitions. Generally speaking, a domestic partnership is defined as two individuals of the same gender who are in a committed relationship of indefinite duration with an exclusive mutual commitment similar to that of marriage. The partners share the necessities of life and agree to be financially responsible for each other's well-being, including living expenses. It should be noted that domestic partners are not married to anyone else, and do not have another domestic partner. Domestic partners may not be related by blood. (Resolution regarding domestic partners, approved by the University of Minnesota Board of Regents September 10, 1993.)

22 *Registered partnership:* A registered partnership is similar to a civil union (see above) in that it too creates a legal partners' relationship. Registered partnerships, like domestic partnerships, grant only some of the benefits of marriage (while Vermont's civil unions give all the state-provided benefits of marriage, but none of the over one thousand federal ones).

23 "Brother Outsider: The Life of Bayard Rustin" is a documentary first aired on PBS January 20th, 2003: Martin Luther King, Jr. Day. "Brother Outsider" is "A Question Why Films" LLC production, made in asso-ciation with Independent Television Service, National Black Program-ming Coalition. Produced by Nancy Kates, Bennett Singer. Executive producer, Sam Pollard. Co-producer, Mridu Chandra. Associate producer, Heather Seldes. Copies available (2003) from California Newsreel, Bur-lington VT, 877-811-7495; 800-621-6196.

24 NCBI is the National Coalition Building Institute. NCBI is a non-profit leadership training organization. Its mission statement reads:

> The National Coalition Building Institute is dedicated to ending the mistreatment of every group whether it stems from nationality, race, class, gender, religion, sexual orientation, age, physical ability, job, or life circumstance. The world is entering an historic new period that re-quires bold and courageous leadership. All of the programs of the National Coalition Building Institute aim to develop this new kind of leader: one who initiates diversity programs, takes principled and cou-rageous stands, can enter the heat of emotional group conflict and build bridges, and models being a fierce ally for *all* groups. NCBI trains com-munity leaders from every field in the skills of prejudice reduction, intergroup conflict resolution, and coalition building. NCBI trained leaders work together in multicultural teams and empower others to eliminate the harmful effects of institutionalized discrimination, ena-bling groups from diverse backgrounds to work together toward shared goals.

NCBI programs "emphasize a train-the-trainer approach whereby every NCBI trained leader, from a fifth grader in elementary school to an elected official in the federal government, is taught how to replicate a set of learned skills and thereby train and empower others." NCBI: 1835 K Street NW, Suite 715, Washington, DC, 20006; (202) 785-9400, FAX (202) 785-3385.

25 This information was also provided by the Alaska Network on Domestic Violence and Sexual Assault in Juneau, in November, 1993, in answer to research questions I posed as I prepared a letter for publication in the *Juneau Empire.*

26 The untrue myth that homosexuals are "the" pedophiles is still deeply embedded and hard to shake. Two footnotes from an article in the *Duke Journal of Gender Law and Policy* (from Duke University Law School,

Terry Sanford Institute of Public Policy, and Duke Graduate Program in Women's Studies) are provided here for readers' further research. These footnotes are from the article "Adoption by Lesbian and Gay People: the Use and Mis-Use of Social Science Research" by Marc E. Elovitz [Fna], © 1995. Cited as 2 *Duke J. Gender L. & Pol'y* 207; Volume 2, 1995; Index; Gay & Lesbian Adoption:

> FN55. Nicholas Groth, Patterns of Sexual Assault Against Children and Adolescents, in Sexual Assault of Children and Adolescents 4 (Ann W. Burgess et al. eds., 1978) ('(T)he belief that homosexuals are particularly attracted to children is completely unsupported by our data.'). See also John Boswell, Christianity, Social Tolerance, and Homosexuality 16 (1980) (explaining that accusations of child molestation have historically been made against disfavored minorities vulnerable to such 'propaganda,' be they gay people, Jews or others); Gregory M. Herek, Myths About Sexual Orientation: A Lawyer's Guide to Social Science Research, 1 Law & Sexuality 133, 156 (1991) (reviewing the literature relating to adult sexual orientation and molestation of children and concluding that gay men are not more likely than heterosexual men to molest children).

> FN56. See Carole Jenny et al., 'Are Children at Risk for Sexual Abuse by Homosexuals?,' 94 Pediatrics 41, 44 (1994) (finding that a child is 100 times more likely to be sexually abused by the heterosexual partner of a relative than by a gay adult); Sam Houston State Univ., Criminal Justice Center, Responding to Child Sexual Abuse: A Report to the 67th Session of the Texas Legislature 22 (1980) (illustrating the vast majority of sex crimes committed by adults upon children are heterosexual, not homosexual).

27 National Coming Out Day (NCOD) happens every October 11th and marks the anniversary of the 1987 "March on Washington" for lesbian-bi-gay-transgender rights. Around the world, individuals, organizations, student groups, etc., mark October 11th as a day to come out to more people, and/or to participate in local coming out events.

28 See the book *Soldier of the Year: The Story of a Gay American Patriot* by Jose Zuniga, Tom Miller (Editor). Publisher: Pocket Star; (October 1994). An excerpt from Amazon.com's editorial review says:

> Another in the growing list of testimonies of gays and lesbians dis-criminated against by the U.S. military, this is the story of Zuniga, an army journalist who in 1992 was named the Sixth Army's soldier of the year. Shortly thereafter, he came out and was discharged for his pains. His basic story is by now all too common; discrimination and prejudice in the military are as stereotypical and patterned as discrimination and prejudice in all the other walks of life.

References

American Academy of Pediatrics. Technical Report: "Coparent or Second-Parent Adoption by Same-Sex Parents." Ellen C. Perrin, MD, and the Committee on Psychosocial Aspects of Child and Family Health. *Pediatrics*, Volume 109, Number 2, February 2002, pp 341-344.

American Psychiatric Association (APA). "Position Statement on Homosexuality and Civil Rights." *American Psychiatry* (April 1974):131:4.

Associated Press. "A look at gay marriage in some countries." *San Francisco Chronicle*. March 4, 2004.

Beeman, William O. Dept. of Anthropology, Brown University. "Marriage Between a 'Man and a Woman' is not so Clear Cut." *Baltimore Sun*, March 17, 1996.

Bloom, Amy. "The Body Lies." *The New Yorker*. July 18, 1994.

Bisexual Resource Center, "Bisexuality" pamphlet. http://www.biresource.org/.

Blumenfeld, Warren J., ed. *Homophobia: How We All Pay the Price*. Boston: Beacon Press, 1992.

Boesser, Rev. Mark and Mildred. "Another Christian Point of View." Editorial. *Juneau Empire*. September 26, 2002. Rev. Mark Boesser is an Episcopal priest and Archdeacon of Southeast Alaska; Mildred Boesser is a founding member of the Juneau Human Rights Commission. Both are founding members of PFLAG-Juneau.

Boesser, Mildred. Testifying before the City Assembly in Anchorage, Alaska. 1989.

Boesser, Sara. "Everyone Can Come Out." Editorial. *Juneau Empire*. October 4, 1988. "Marriage, biblical teachings not threatened by domestic partners." Editorial. *Juneau Empire*. December 17, 2003.

Breedlove, Marc S., University of California Berkley. Reviewing the book *Sexing the Body: Gender Politics and the Construction of Sexuality*. By Anne Fausto-Sterling. By New York Basic Books, 2000.

Bryant, Suzanne. Press release. "Judges' Code May Include Ban on Discrimination Against Gays." The National Lesbian and Gay Law Association. Boston, MA. September 22, 1989.

Buxton, Amity Pierce. *The Other Side of the Closet: the Coming Out Crisis for Straight Spouses.* Santa Monica, CA: IBS Press, Inc. 1991.

Cabaj, Dr. Robert Paul, M.D. Letter to Anchorage, Alaska, Equal Rights Commission. Explains American Psychiatric Association's support for equal rights for homosexuals. He was a former Chair of the Committee on Gay, Lesbian and Bisexual Issues of the APA. February 24, 1990.

Chicago Defender, "Coretta Scott King Compares Gay Rights and African-American Civil Rights Movements." April 1, 1998. Excerpt republished at Hatecrimes.org, January 2003.

Data Lounge, http://www.datalounge.com/, "Civil Unions Fade as Political Issue." Montpelier, Vermont. November 27, 2002.

Diamond, John. "Gays in the military found better suited than average." *San Francisco Examiner.* October 29, 1989.

Dignan, Joe and Sanchez, Rene. "San Francisco Opens Marriage to Gay Couples." *Washington Post,* February 13, 2004)

Elovitz, Marc E. "Adoption by Lesbian and Gay People: The Use and Mis-Use of Social Science Research." *Duke Journal of Gender Law and Policy,* an interdisciplinary journal, Duke University Law School, Terry Sanford Institute of Public Policy, and Duke Graduate Program in Women's Studies. Cite as 2 Duke J. Gender L. & Pol'y 207. Volume 2, 1995; Index; Gay & Lesbian Adoption. Duke University Law School, Durham, NC, 1995.

Fleer, Nigel. "Imprint Online: Human-Outlook." Friday, May 19, 2000. Volume 23, Number 2.

GenderPac: Gender Public Advocacy Coalition. "Myth vs. Fact about Gender Stereotypes." 2003.

Genel, Myron. "Gender Verification No More?" Medscape Women's Health eJournal[TM], Volume 7, Number 6. 2002.

Gibson, Paul. Chapter titled "Gay Male and Lesbian Youth Suicide" in the "Report of the Secretary's Task Force on Youth Suicide," published by the United States Department of Health & Human Services, Public Health Service; Alcohol, Drug Abuse and Mental Health Administration. DHHS Publication No. (ADM)89-1623. Rockville, MD, 1989.

Green, Melissa S. and Jay K. Brause. *Identity Reports: Sexual Orientation Bias in Alaska.* Identity, Inc., Anchorage, AK, 1989.

Groth, A. Nicholas & Birnbaum, B. "Adult Sexual Orientation and Attraction to Underage Persons." *Archives of Sexual Behavior* 7:175181, 1978. (A. Nicholas Groth: Director of the Sex Offender Program, Connecticut Department of Corrections, CoDirector of the St. Joseph College Institute for the Treatment and Control of Child Sexual Abuse.)

Guilbeault, Matt. "Intersexism in Sports: A Human Rights Issue." Internet: http://members.fortunecity.com/dikigoros/intersexism.htm. 1998-1999.

Hatecrimes.org: "Coretta Scott King Compares Gay Rights and African-American Civil Rights Movements." January, 2003.

Heredia, Christopher. "Proud mom of hero—She'll march in gay fete to honor son on Flight 93." *San Francisco Chronicle.* Staff Writer. June 28, 2002.

Holmes, M. Morgan. Paper. "Queer Cut Bodies: Intersexuality and Homophobia in Medical Practice." Internet; Yahoo; topic: "Intersexual Society:" Concordia University, Alberta, Canada, 1995.

Hosek, Linda. "Same-Sex Debate Unable to Settle 'Equality'—Adoption expert rejects state's hypothetical search for optimal child development." *Honolulu Star-Bulletin.* September 19, 2001.

Human Rights Campaign Foundation. "What child welfare and health experts say about gay, lesbian, bisexual and transgender parenting." Also: "Winning Domestic Partner Benefits." And "Same-Sex Marriage and Civil Unions." http://www.hrc.org/, 2003.

Identity, Inc. "One in Ten: A Profile of Alaska's Lesbian & Gay Community." Report prepared by the volunteers of Identity, Inc. Anchorage, AK 1986.

International Foundation for Gender Education, www.ifge.org.

Intersex Society of North America (ISNA). Homepage: http://www.isna.org/.

Jones, Charisse. "Poll: Young Adults back gay marriages." *USA Today.* July 1, 2003.

King, Coretta Scott. Remarks, press conference in support of Employment Non-Discrimination Act, ENDA: a bill to add employment protection regardless of sexual orientation. Washington D.C. June 23, 1994. Online in 2003 at hatecrimes.org.

Kinsey, Alfred C. et al. *Sexual Behavior in the Human Male.* Philadelphia: W.B. Saunders; Bloomington, IN: Indiana U. Press, 1948. And *Sexual Behavior in the Human Female,* Philadelphia: W.B. Saunders; Bloomington, IN: Indiana U. Press, 1953.

Koch, Dr. Patricia Barthalow, Ph.D. "Exploring Sexual Orientation," Curriculum, Penn State University, 1987. Dr. Koch is Associate Professor of Bio-behavioral Health, Penn State University, in 2004.

Lambda Legal Defense and Education Fund. "International Recognition of Same-Sex Partnerships—Marriage Project Fact Sheet." March 30, 2001.

Leydon, Joe. "PBS Honors Unsung Civil Rights Hero." *Reuters,* January 17, 2003. (Documentary, "Brother Outsider: The Life of Bayard Rustin.")

Massachusetts Department of Education. Report. "1995 Massachusetts Youth Risk Behavior Survey Results." The Massachusetts Governor's Commission on Gay and Lesbian Youth publications are free of charge. http://www.state.ma.us/gcgly/PublicationsoftheCommission.html, 2003.

McCain, U.S. Senator John (R-Arizona). Press release: "Eulogy in Honor of Mark Bingham." Delivered by Senator John McCain, San Francisco, CA, September 22, 2001. http://mccain.senate.gov/index.cfm?fuseaction=Newscenter.ViewPressRelease&Content_id=213.

Meade, Michael, J. "Gay Bishop: 'The Church Will Survive.'" 365Gay.com. October 20, 2003.

Mollenkott, Virginia Ramey. *Omnigender: A Trans-Religious Approach.* The Pilgrim Press. 2001. And co-auther with Letha Dawson Scanzoni: *Is the Homosexual My Neighbor? Another Christian View.* 1978. Reprint, *Is the Homosexual My Neighbor? A Positive Christian Response.* HarperSan-Francisco, 1994.

Murray, Frank J. "High court to rule on sodomy laws." *The Washington Times.* December 2, 2002.

National Coalition Building Institute (NCBI). 1835 K Street NW, Suite 715, Washington, DC, 20006; (202) 785-9400, FAX (202) 785-3385. Provides prejudice reduction and coalition building workshops for schools, government services, businesses and organizations internationally.

Ontario Consultants on Religious Tolerance, "Legal and Economic Benefits of Marriage." ("The list [of benefits] was compiled for a couple living in the United States. However, similar provisions exist in many other countries.") ReligiousTolerance.org, 2003.

Oregonian. Editorial. "No shield from predators: parents shouldn't assume that Measure 9 would rid schools of potential sexual abusers." Portland, Oregon. September 18, 1992.

Parents, Families and Friends of Lesbians and Gays (PFLAG). A U.S. national organization with many local chapters. It provides support, education, and advocacy for sexual minority people and for their family and friends. PFLAG provides a newspaper and a comprehensive list of books, articles, cassettes, and video tapes designed for understanding homosexual, bisexual, transgender, and intersexual persons' lives. To locate the nearest PFLAG chapter or help-line in the U.S. or Canada, call 202-467-8180 (v); 202-638-0243 (fax); web: www.pflag.org/; email: info@pflag.org; Mail: PFLAG, 1726 M Street NW, Suite 400, Washington, DC 20036.

Pawlowski, Wayne V., ACSW, LICSW. Consultant, Trainer, Clinical Social Worker and Former Director of Training for Planned Parenthood Federation of America. Email: WaynePawlowski@aol.com, Arlington, Virginia. References are to his workshop for teachers and counselors "Understanding Sexuality in Our Society." Co-sponsored by the Alaska Department of Education and the federal Alaska Cooperative Extension Service. Juneau, Alaska. 1990.

Price, Deb and Murdoch, Joyce (Contributor). *And Say Hi to Joyce.* Doubleday, 1997.

Preves, Sharon E. "For the Sake of the Children: Destigmatizing Intersexuality." From *Intersex in the Age of Ethics; Ethics in Clinical Medicine Series.* Edited by Alice Domurat Dreger. University Publishing Group, Hagerstown, Maryland. 1999.

Project/Project Interaction, McGill University. The project's 2003 mission statement begins: "Project/Project Interaction is committed to the health and well-being of gay, lesbian, bisexual and two-spirited (glbt-s) people, their families, communities and allies. . . . "

Reuters. "Coretta Scott King Compares Gay Rights and African-American Civil Rights Movements." March 31, 1998. (Online at Hatecrimes.org January 2003).

Reinisch, June M., with Ruth Beasley. *The Kinsey Institute New Report on Sex.* New York: St. Martin's Press, 1990.

Robinson, Bruce A. Paper. "Female and Intersexual Genital Mutilation in North America." Ontario Consultants on Religious Tolerance. Ontario, Canada, 1997.

Saewyc E.M., Bearinger L.H., Blum R.W., Resnick M.D. "Sexual intercourse, abuse and pregnancy among adolescent women: Does sexual orientation make a difference?" *Family Planning Perspectives,* 31(3), 127-131, 1999.

Scanzoni, Letha Dawson, and Virginia Ramey Mollenkott. *Is the Homosexual My Neighbor? Another Christian View.* 1978. Reprinted as *Is the Homosexual My Neighbor? A Positive Christian Response.* HarperSanFrancisco, 1994.

Stacey, Judith and Timothy Biblarz. *American Sociological Review,* "(How) Does the Sexual Orientation of Parents Matter?" Vol. 66 (April: 159-183) 2001.

Straight Spouse Network (SSN), www.ssnetwk.org/.

Sullivan, Andrew. "The GOP Divide On Gay Marriage." *Washington Post.* December 7, 2003.

Thompson, Cooper. "On Being Heterosexual in a Homophobic World." *Homophobia: How We All Pay the Price* Editor: Warren J. Blumenfeld. Boston: Beacon Press, 1992.

TIME Magazine, front cover. "Yep, I'm Gay." The cover was due to Ellen DeGeneres coming out in her personal life and on her television series "Ellen." In "Ellen," on April 30, 1997, she made history when the lead character, Ellen Morgan, came out in "The Puppy Episode." On *TIME* Magazine's cover: April 14, 1997.

United States. Department of Health & Human Services, Public Health Service; Alcohol, Drug Abuse and Mental Health Administration. "Report of the Secretary's Task Force on Youth Suicide." By Paul Gibson. DHHS Publication No. (ADM)89-1623. Rockville, MD, 1989.

USA Today. "Coretta Scott King gives her support to gay marriage." March 24, 2004.

Wartik, Nancy. "Jerry's Choice: Why Are Our Children Killing Themselves?" *American Health—Fitness of Body and Mind. Reader's Digest Publications,* New York, October 1991.

Wald, Michael S. "Same-Sex Couples: Marriage, Families, and Children." Law Professor, Stanford University. Working Paper No. 6. Social Science Research Network Electronic Paper Collection. 1999. http://papers.ssrn.com/sol3/delivery.cfm/000111401.pdf?abstractid=203649 .

Washington Post. "No Gay Help Wanted." *The Press Room,* November 20, 2002. Available online at website for Servicemembers Legal Defense Network, http://www.sldn.org/ in 2003.

Whealin, Julie. National Center for PTSD Fact Sheet: "Child Sexual Abuse." http://www.ncptsd.org/facts/specific/fs_child_sexual_abuse.html, 2002.

Whoriskey, Peter. "A New Year's Baby With an Additional Difference: 2 Moms." *Washington Post* Staff Writer. January 2, 2003.

Wikholm, Andrew. "Word List; Words: Queer." www.Gayhistory.com. 1999.

Wink, Walter. "Homosexuality and the Bible." *Christian Century Magazine.* 1979, Christian Century Foundation; Reprinted by permission: 1996 by Walter Wink.

Witeck-Combs Communications/Harris Interactive Survey. "Fewer than Half Of All Lesbian, Gay, Bisexual and Transgender Adults Surveyed Say They have Disclosed Their Sexual Orientation to Their Health Care Provider." Dec. 17, 2002.

Zorn, Eric. "Marriage issue just as plain as black and white." *Chicago Tribune,* ericzorn@aol.com. May 19, 1996.

Zuniga, Jose. *Soldier of the Year: The Story of a Gay American Patriot.* Tom Miller, Editor. Pocket Star, 1994.

Index

About the Author

Sara L. Boesser lives in Juneau, Alaska, and is a graduate of the University of Washington. She is a human rights advocate who has received numerous awards for her work for equal rights for all regardless of sexual orientation and for equal access for people who experience disabilities. She has been featured in several books to date, among them *Making History: the Struggle for Gay and Lesbian Equal Rights* and *Is it a Choice?* both by Eric Marcus; and in an anthology titled *Side by Side: On Having a Gay or Lesbian Sibling,* edited by Andrew R. Gottlieb, Ph.D.